THE CIVIL SERVICE COMMISSION

DONALD R. HARVEY

Foreword by JOHN W. MACY, Jr.

More than 2.5 million men and women make up the civilian work force of the U.S. Government today. They perform every conceivable kind of work, not only in Washington, D.C., home base of the giant bureaucracy, but also in the most remote parts of the country and around the world as well. Each year, some 3 million people are examined for possible entry into this huge force. Small wonder that the Civil Service Commission, the agency charged with regulating and supervising government hiring, advancement, pay, discharge, and conditions of employment, has often been a storm center.

The Commission, as the author of this book informs us, is always busy, always involved to some degree in every phase of federal activity, and is "caught in a continuous crossfire of pressures, demands, and issues." Its problems "range from those caused by the sympathetic intercession of influential persons for individuals in need of help to those resulting from massive group action in behalf of a major policy."

The history of the civil service has been one of unending struggle over how government job appointments are made. The Commission was created by the Pendleton Act of 1883, after a period in American history that was marked by the astonishing excesses of the "spoils system." But, even though the Commission's powers and resources have been extended by subsequent legislation, the struggle for the supremacy of merit over political favoritism is by no means wholly won. Only recently has the Commission come into its own in the highest councils of government. During the Kennedy Administration, it assumed a much broader personnel-management role than it had held before. Donald Harvey gives credit for

The Civil Service Commission

Donald R. Harvey

FOREWORD BY

JOHN W. MACY, JR.

PRAEGER PUBLISHERS

New York · Washington · London

PRAEGER PUBLISHERS
111 Fourth Avenue, New York, N.Y. 10003, U.S.A.
5, Cromwell Place, London S.W.7, England

Published in the United States of America in 1970
by Praeger Publishers, Inc.

© 1970 by Donald R. Harvey

Library of Congress Catalog Card Number: 72–78919

This book is No. 19 in the series
Praeger Library of U.S. Government Departments and Agencies

Printed in the United States of America

To my

much of the Commission's new influence and prominence to former Chairman John W. Macy, Jr., who served in both the Kennedy and Johnson administrations and, as the author says, took "as challenge and charter" words spoken by President John F. Kennedy in his first state of the Union message: "Let the public service be a proud and lively career."

Mr. Harvey's own consuming interest in public service, and in the Commission he himself served for fourteen years, is apparent on every page of this informative book. He discusses with unusual insight not only the history of the Commission but also its current organization and specific functions; its relationships with other agencies of government, with Congress, and with various special-interest groups; its delicate problems with enforcement of regulations; its affect on, and (sometimes admittedly slow) response to, broad changes in policy; and, throughout, its prickly working partnership with the Post Office Department.

Valuable appendixes show the civil service regions of the United States, list U.S. civil service commissioners since 1883, detail the Pendleton Act and other applicable laws, and describe career opportunities in personnel management, in the Commission, and elsewhere in government.

THE AUTHOR: Donald R. Harvey, now a personnel-management consultant in Washington, D.C., entered the federal civil service immediately after graduating from the University of Nebraska in 1934. His government career included service in several agencies, among them the Bureau of the Budget, the Department of Agriculture, the Office of War Information, and the Civil Aeronautics Administration; in both of the latter, he held the position of personnel director. In 1952, he joined the Civil Service Commission and, from 1962 to 1966, was director of the Commission's Bureau of Recruiting and Examining.

Foreword

by JOHN W. MACY, JR.
Chairman, U.S. Civil Service Commission, 1961–69

Government is people. A democratic government must be a response to the will of its people. And, to be truly responsive, such a government must serve its citizens through the skills and dedication of the people who work for it. The Civil Service Commission has been the principal instrument whereby those who serve the people are recruited and selected, developed and motivated, rewarded and disciplined. Since its creation by Congress in 1883, the Commission as an institution has evolved to meet the needs of the American people and their government. This evolution has accelerated in recent times as the nation has become larger, more complex, and more responsive to the people's needs.

The story of the Commission is, therefore, a very human story. It is a story of men and women, not just policies and procedures. It is a story that can be told only by a narrator who has been actively engaged in the work of the Commission and has known its problems, its successes, and its failures at first hand. Donald Harvey is such a person. He has experienced the responsibility of directing the Commission's most basic program—the recruitment and examination of men and women under the principles of the merit system. He has a keen eye and an accurate ear for the comedies and the tragedies in this aspect of the people's business.

In this book, Donald Harvey tells the tale of a government institution dedicated to better government through the presence of excellence in the ranks of those who serve their government. His words reveal the validity of President Kennedy's famous description of public service as "proud and lively." Donald Harvey's book should eliminate certain popular myths concerning civil service and should demonstrate that the individual is still a precious asset, even to a government that employs millions.

As a partisan of the public service and a constant advocate of the merit system, I hope that the readers of this volume will be encouraged to contribute their talents to the general welfare for at least part of their working lives.

Preface

In 1952, when I was privileged to join the staff of the U.S. Civil Service Commission, the Commission announced the fact to the press. Although it was not the most exciting news story of the day, it did get around, and it inspired my oldest brother to write me a letter that began, "Dear Mr. R.F.D." To him, the Civil Service Commission meant the postal service and some hotly contested races for the position of rural letter carrier that we had known as boys.

Sometime later, when I was visiting my home town in Missouri, an old acquaintance inquired about what I was doing for a living. When I responded that I was working for the Civil Service Commission in Washington, he said, "Oh, I have a friend in the civil service. I wonder if you might know him?" It turned out that the friend was a railway mail clerk working out of St. Louis, and my chances of knowing him were about as remote as those of knowing any citizen of St. Louis selected at random.

These unrelated episodes helped convince me that the role of the Civil Service Commission as an institution, separate from the broad category of government workers known as the civil service, was not widely understood. Although the intervening years and the communications media have done much to broaden the general knowledge of the Commission, I have continued to be troubled by the feeling that it is not understood well enough. Hence, in the pages that follow, I have endeavored to write about the Commission as I have known it—as a human institution reflecting the problems, abilities, successes, and failures of the people who have manned it since its establishment in 1883. If this presentation causes the Commission to take on something of the image of a person, then to me that seems appropriate. For, in its actions, the Commission struggles for perfection but falls short of its goals just as people do, because, like them, it exists in an imperfect society.

When one writes a book about an institution with which he has been closely associated for many years, he must try to make certain that his work reflects whatever unique knowledge the association has given him without being slanted too much by his personal experience. To correct my own prejudices, I spent much time checking with my former colleagues at the Commission. They helped me maintain the role of reporter, not advocate, and to them I am deeply indebted. Covering briefly programs or projects that could be subjects of entire books presented another problem. In this connection, I wish to make it plain that, although the staff of the Commission supplied much of the material upon which this book is based, I am solely responsible for the opinions expressed in it and the manner in which the story is told.

So many people at the Commission gave me assistance that it is impossible for me to list them all. However, the assistance of some people was of such significance that I must mention them. Certainly, I am deeply indebted to John W. Macy, Jr., one of Washington's busiest men, not only for writing the Foreword but also for giving me much help and encouragement. Commissioners Ludwig J. Andolsek and Robert E. Hampton kept their doors open to me, as did Executive Director Nicholas J. Oganovic. O. Glenn Stahl was an enthusiastic and able consultant who made many valuable suggestions. David F. Williams and Philip W. Schulte were always coop-

erative and helpful. I suppose that one is likely to impose the
most on those with whom he has been associated the longest.
I am sure I was guilty of that fault, in calling so frequently on
Betty F. Walker, John E. Beckman, and Donald F. Biglin for
help. They responded as though we were still on the same
payroll and told me when they thought I was wrong—just as
they always had.

I also received assistance from many people outside the
Commission. Special thanks are due Betty Lu Lowry, who provided important information on many of the incidents related
and who also gave me fine editorial assistance, in addition to
typing much of the manuscript. My old friends Hugh and
Martha Gauch and Robert and Helen Carey read copy as
outsiders, unfamiliar with either the concerns or the language
of the federal bureaucrat. They raised questions that caused
me to reconsider much of what I had written, and they encouraged me to do the rewriting that their questions dictated.

To all these and many others, I am deeply grateful. I hope
the results adequately reflect the value of their contributions.

Adelphi, Maryland
August, 1969

Contents

A section of photographs follows page 82.

*A chart on page 38 shows the organization of the U.S. Civil
Service Commission.*

The Civil Service Commission

I

A Central
Personnel Agency Develops

"The lengthened shadow of a man," Ralph Waldo Emerson's definition of an institution, cannot be applied with accuracy to the U.S. Civil Service Commission. Not even the fact that one of its earliest commissioners was a courageous Theodore Roosevelt who took on all comers in defense of the merit system can alter such a conclusion. So many other men and women of diverse abilities and motivations and so many circumstances have affected its growth and character that no one individual or event can be cited as having been most influential in establishing the agency as it is today. Indeed, it now has an institutional personality so complex that it is one of Washington's least understood agencies. The Commission's fundamental role today is to establish and maintain a dynamic policy of personnel administration based on the principle of merit for the federal civilian workforce of more than 2.5 million employees.

Financially poor and not fully acceptable in the bureaucratic society of Washington for most of its more than fourscore years, the Civil Service Commission has recently reached a position of influence and prestige unknown in former years. Achievement of this status, however, was not accomplished singlehandedly or without difficulty. External pressures and circumstances over which the Commission had relatively little control contributed in great measure to its development as the central personnel agency in name and in fact for the country's largest employer, the U.S. Government.

There were times in its history when it seemed to resist the forces that moved to strengthen it. Its career has been somewhat like that of a gifted child from whom much was expected but who encountered great difficulty in living up to his potential. When the Commission reached an age at which it should have been ready for the challenges and responsibilities of its time, its performance was considered inadequate. There were those who, in disappointment, would have given up and abandoned it. Others, however, insisted that it be required to play its proper role in society. The latter point of view prevailed, forcing it to grow in capacity and performance.

THE SPOILS SYSTEM

To understand the Commission and its role in today's government, it is necessary briefly to review significant legislative developments pertaining to federal employment. Rarely has the United States passed a law or taken an action in anticipation of a problem that may occur; too frequently it has waited until forced to curb an already flagrant abuse. Such was the case with the establishment of the Civil Service Commission, created in crisis to stamp out the evils of using the federal job as a payoff to someone, perhaps not even the appointee, for services rendered.

Although the removal and replacement of federal jobholders by an incoming administration did not begin with the election of Andrew Jackson in 1828, it was his Administration that was credited with adopting the practice as a principle—if one may call it that—of improving public administration.

The upheaval that brought Jackson into power carried with it loud cries for "throwing the rascals out"—one of the great clichés of the American political heritage. Earlier administrations had placed persons from the well-to-do, better-educated segments of the population in federal jobs. The Jackson Administration was vulnerable to arguments for "democratizing" the service and making it more representative of all citizens. Jackson himself, though apparently not as spoils-minded as some members of his Administration, stated that the "duties of all public offices are, or at least admit of being made, so plain and simple that men of intelligence may qualify themselves for their performance." He also said, "I cannot but believe that more is lost by long continuance of men in office than is generally gained by their experience." After the Jacksonian era, the spoils system was embraced to such an extent and hiring practices became so deplorable that the fiber of the federal government was undoubtedly weakened. Periodic rotation in office to provide a fresh, responsive, and representative workforce became the window dressing for a course of action that made jobs the property of the party victorious in an election, and, although some of its sponsors may have been sincerely motivated, the avaricious, for many years thereafter, looked upon the government job as legal tender in the realm of political exchange. It was considered a requisite of party organization and discipline.

The phrase "to the victors belong the spoils" now seems so self-condemning when applied to the filling of federal jobs that one wonders how it could ever have been publicly tolerated. It had, nevertheless, been so widely accepted across the country that it was generally considered one of the rules of the game. If there were many who recognized it as an evil to be stamped out, they were not sufficiently influential or articulate to arouse the voters.

During the Lincoln Administration, pressure by jobseekers constituted a serious interference with the prosecution of the Civil War. So brazen were their importunities that they actually invaded the executive mansion itself. Histories of the era make frequent reference to the problem (and to Lincoln's vexation); they paint a ludicrous picture of the President's having to elbow his way through crowds of jobseekers clamoring for his attention in the White House corridors when he was en route from his office to dinner. Once, when Lincoln was suffering from an attack of smallpox, he asked an assistant to invite the jobseekers in, for at last he had something he could give to all of them.

The miserable pressures and responsibilities that the spoils system put on the Chief Executive are blamed for the deaths of two Presidents. President James A. Garfield was assassinated by a disappointed jobseeker in 1881. William Henry Harrison's death, four decades earlier, has been attributed to illness resulting from overwork in maintaining an exhausting schedule dealing with the jobseekers during the first weeks of his Administration.

In the years immediately after the Civil War, the forces of reform began to develop and the idea of establishing a merit system gained adherents. However, the ground swell of support from the people, essential to achievement of congressional action, was slow to come.

The first meaningful course of action, though destined for a short life, began in 1870 when the secretaries of the Interior and the Treasury, by means of departmental orders, introduced merit procedures for filling certain positions. In the same year, President Ulysses S. Grant asked Congress for legislation to govern the making of appointments and called attention to the long-standing abuses. A number of bills were introduced, but none were enacted. Finally, on March 3, 1871, by a rider on an appropriation bill, the President was authorized to prescribe regulations for admission into the civil service and to determine the fitness of each candidate. Under this authorization, President Grant appointed the first Civil Service Commission, which then consisted of seven members, and the first competitive examination under its direction was held in April, 1872. However, in 1873, Congress refused to appropriate further funds for the function, and the organization was completely abandoned in 1875.

Although continued interest in civil service reform was

manifested by private citizens and groups, Congress maintained an attitude of disinterest. The concept of patronage as an essential political tool in party organization and control was so firmly entrenched that it was not easy to give it up.

THE CIVIL SERVICE ACT

After the assassination of President Garfield, the reform movement gained momentum, rolling over both apathy and opposition and resulting in the passage of the Pendleton Act in 1883—the basic legislation establishing the Civil Service Commission, under which the merit system is conducted today. Better known as the Civil Service Act, it was entitled "An Act to Regulate and Improve the Civil Service of the United States." It enabled the President to make rules governing the filling of positions, and it required that they be filled "from among those graded highest" in examinations, insofar as "conditions of good administration will warrant." It authorized the establishment of a bipartisan commission of three members to aid the President in carrying out the provisions of the Act.

Although its framers were farsighted concerning the kind of law that could endure, they did not foresee the need to provide adequate resources to enable the Commission to do its job. In addition to the three commissioners, the only staff provided for was a chief examiner, a secretary, a stenographer, and a messenger. The Act specified that the Secretary of the Interior would supply space, stationery, and other necessary articles for the Commission. By implication, at least, it said that, except for work related to the immediate duties of the commissioners, duties would be performed by employees of other federal agencies. Consequently, the stage was set for the Commission's having to rely upon the cooperation of others, rather than its own staff, to get its job done, thus creating a problem that has haunted the Commission to the present day.

By 1890, dissatisfaction was growing within the Commission over its inability to get the agencies to supply the necessary manpower. The Commission began submitting requests and obtaining appropriations for a staff of its own, although much work continued to be performed by personnel on the various federal agency rolls. Through the years, however, the Commission suffered from lack of a consistent financial program properly related to the current staffing problems of the total federal service that it was expected to serve.

The Civil Service Act specifically required immediate coverage under the merit system only of certain positions in the Post Office and Treasury departments, representing a small percentage of the total positions in the executive branch. Its message was strong, however. The number was to be enlarged as the President, with the advice of the Commission, determined enlargement to be feasible. This placed the Commission in the role of missionary, with a large population to convert while having to rely on the help of the same population to get the job done.

The problem of installing a merit system and eliminating the widespread abuses foreordained the Commission to a life of questionable popularity in the federal agencies among which it had to live. It was expected to control their actions by regulating the manner in which they filled jobs. It would be required to apply restraints, which administrators undoubtedly would find annoying even though they might not disagree with the objective. So entrenched were the old practices of favoritism that primary emphasis had to be placed on what was illegal under the new law, thus establishing a reputation that was to give the Commission trouble in later years.

The bipartisan nature of the Commission and its role as the public protector of the merit system were to give it an aloofness from the other federal agencies, and even from the Chief Executive, that caused public-administration students to engage in continuing debate over its role—whether it was an

independent agency primarily reporting to Congress or an
arm of the President. *[handwritten annotation]*

EXPANSION OF THE FEDERAL MERIT SYSTEM

In spite of its lack of popularity with professional politicians, the merit system experienced slow but steady expansion
in the years following 1883 and the passage of the Pendleton
Act. Starting with the initial coverage of 10.5 per cent of
government positions, or approximately 13,780 jobs, succes-
sive administrations increased the percentage to 79.6, or 426,-
083 jobs, by 1930. Some administrations carried out positive
programs of expanding the system; others either were lethar-
gic or actually took actions that led away from the merit system. Opposition to the concept of merit was rarely voiced,
however. To have done so would have been to register a
public endorsement of sin. Even though it was popular to
give at least lip service in support of the merit principle, some
administrations were less aggressive than others in their efforts
to expand it. In spite of the uneven performance of the various administrations and some relatively minor setbacks, advance was steady.

In a number of instances, expansion was by "blanketing-
in" near the end of an Administration—that is to say, by the
placing of a job under the competitive service, permitting the
incumbent to retain it, and, in so doing, acquire full civil
service status. Such actions frequently led to controversy over
whether their real motive was to improve government by
extending the merit principle to more jobs or to give job
security to the party faithful and remove a plum from the
reach of the opposition party about to assume office. Whatever the motivation, once jobs were covered under the merit
system, they were rarely to be uncovered.

Although the practice was not uniform in earlier years,
today an employee blanketed-in is required to qualify in a

noncompetitive examination appropriate to the specific job. Employees with civil service status are protected from arbitrary removal, political or otherwise. In addition, they may move between and within agencies to jobs for which they qualify without participating in competitive examinations open to the public, and, if they leave government service, they may re-enter noncompetitively. Also, when reductions in the workforce are made, they are retained in preference to non-status employees with similar skills.

The Beginning of Modern Personnel Management

The Civil Service Act, having gone a long way toward improving the quality of the federal staff, was nonetheless targeted primarily at eliminating politics and favoritism in filling jobs and at preventing actions against employees for their failure to make campaign contributions. Therefore, it did not cover a number of important areas of personnel administration as we know it today.

After 1900, increased interest in the welfare of employees in all lines of endeavor led to many legislative adventures into the then relatively unknown and untouched area of concern for employees' rights. One such adventure was the Lloyd–LaFollette Act of 1912. By ensuring the right of employees, individually or collectively, to petition Congress and to belong to postal unions so long as they did not strike, it provided the foundation for today's extensive employee organizations. It also required that agencies follow formal procedures when removing an employee by first giving him a written notice of reasons and then allowing him time to answer.

During the 1920's, two pieces of important personnel legislation were enacted by Congress. In recognition of a long-standing need, the Civil Service Retirement Act was passed in 1920, establishing a retirement and annuity schedule (see Chapter IV). In 1923, the Classification Act was passed to ensure application of the principle of equal pay for equal work and to bring order out of a chaotic pay situation.* Additionally, the jobs in Washington were graded in accordance with the duties and responsibilities of the positions. Positions in the field service were covered by subsequent legislation.

It is significant to note that as new personnel functions were identified, they were not automatically assigned to the Commission. For example, the administration of the Classification Act of 1923 was assigned to a specially created board. It did not become the responsibility of the Civil Service Commission until 1932, and it was not until 1934 that full responsibility for the administration of the Retirement Act was given to the Commission.

THE NEW DEAL

When Franklin D. Roosevelt's Administration began, the government experienced its most significant expansion in any like period of time in history, and most of it took place outside the merit system. Consequently, the early New Deal era was not a particularly bright one for the Civil Service Commission or the merit system it administered. While the number of jobs in government increased greatly, the percentage of jobs covered by the merit system decreased to its lowest in a good many years.

Many believed that staffing the New Deal agencies from outside the competitive service was a patronage raid by the incoming Administration. The issue ignited great controversy at the time, but, when it is viewed in the light of history, one must conclude that more than patronage was involved. The new Administration was staffed with political realists who were no less partisan in their approach than all professional politicians have been. The Republicans had been in office for

---

* The Classification Act of 1923 was superseded and modernized by the Classification Act of 1949, which continued the same principles but extended coverage and clarified responsibilities of the agencies and the Commission.

twenty years, and the Democrats were eager for patronage. But at the same time, government expansion occurred that was more than numerical: the scope of government was greatly increased. The Great Depression had focused attention on so many problems that the federal government was expected to solve that new programs were developed overnight, requiring skills never before utilized by the federal service. There was a great sense of urgency about getting the programs under way with properly motivated personnel.

Also important and not to be overlooked was the capacity and readiness of the Commission to cope with the problem of staffing new agencies on short notice. The Depression had caused such widespread unemployment that all members of Congress and other people of influence were besieged with job applications, many from extremely well qualified people. This occurred at a time when the Commission—not a strong agency to begin with—had been weakened by reductions in appropriations. Lists of persons who had passed examinations were not current, and there had been little opportunity for the many who were unemployed to compete in examinations. Furthermore, demands for jobs were so great that the announcement of any examination resulted in a swamping of the Commission with applications. Even had everyone been enthusiastic about using competitive examining procedures to fill all the jobs being created, indefensible delays would undoubtedly have occurred in launching new programs.

An interesting development of this era is that, although the merit system as it had been known was bypassed, the concept of merit was by no means totally ignored. Some New Deal agencies were established with the most modern personnel management systems Washington had seen. Some agencies required appointees to meet high qualification standards, even though the candidates might also have been required to have the "appropriate" political endorsement. For instance, the Resettlement Administration and its successor, the Farm Security Administration, a large and controversial agency of the day, required its appointees to clerical and stenographic positions to pass written examinations. The politicians knew and understood that candidates had to be qualified, but, since this was not a legal requirement, it would be naïve to assume that there were not instances in which it was waived. Such instances were exceptions rather than the rule, however.

The Farm Security Administration also carried on an annual recruiting program on the agricultural college campuses to build its junior professional staff. Like some of the other agencies, it began operations with a fully organized personnel office under a director of personnel, along the lines of modern industry. To this extent, it was more advanced than many of the so-called old-line agencies.

A notable exception among the older agencies, however, was the Department of Agriculture. It was a pioneer in personnel management and a recognized leader, having one of the most modern and sophisticated personnel offices in Washington.

EMERGENCE OF THE NEED FOR A CENTRAL PERSONNEL AGENCY

Since the passage of the Civil Service Act, there had been two civil services—the "competitive" and the "excepted." The competitive service was comprised of jobs that were subject to competitive examining procedures when filled by appointees from outside the service; the excepted service consisted of jobs not subject to competitive examining requirements. In addition to entire agencies, the excepted service included some jobs in practically every agency. There were laws and policies applying equally to both services, and there were problems common to both.

The Civil Service Commission was generally considered the central personnel agency for the competitive service, having little to do with the excepted service, for which there was no central personnel agency. Even in its own area, the Commission devoted most of its attention to the initial filling of jobs through competitive procedures and left largely to agency management the matter of what happened to personnel on the job.

The problem of the lack of a government-wide central agency had already been recognized. In 1910, President William Howard Taft had unsuccessfully sought approval of Congress to establish a bureau of personnel. In 1931, the Commission recommended in its annual report that all agencies concerned with personnel in the civil service be combined into one agency. President Herbert Hoover approved but went further and recommended that the Commission become an advisory body and that its chairman be named head of a personnel administration under which all the various personnel functions would be grouped. A bill was introduced to implement the proposal but it was never acted on.

In 1936, President Roosevelt established a committee to study the administrative management of the federal government. The committee, headed by the distinguished Louis Brownlow, made many far-reaching recommendations, and some of the most fundamental and significant were in personnel administration.

In its report to the President and Congress in 1937, the Brownlow Committee brought the need for more concentrated attention on problems of personnel management into public view. It called for extension of the merit system "upward, outward, and downward" and recommended the establishment of a new central personnel agency under a single administrator reporting to the President. The committee had studied the Commission and its staff and concluded that it was not then equipped to fulfill the expectations of a central personnel agency. The committee recommended the transfer of the Commission's functions and duties to the proposed new agency. Although the wording of the report did not specifically mention abolishing the Commission, it took no between-the-lines reading to identify that as its objective.

The detailed report of the study conducted by the committee's research staff set forth its reasons for finding that a new central personnel agency was necessary. It concluded that personnel matters received insufficient attention by the Chief Executive, pointing out that the civil service rules had not been given a thorough revision since 1903 and that there were other agencies having central personnel functions, with no coordination beneath the level of the Chief Executive. It also pointed out that "the plural nature of the Commission" contributed to a status of remoteness from the Chief Executive—that it was difficult, if not impossible, for him to have the same direct relationship with the Commission that he had with agencies having a single head. Although one of its members was designated as the Commission's president, each member had an equal voice.

With respect to the Commission's capabilities, the report indicated that: (1) operating agencies felt that the Commission's staff lacked awareness of agency needs and an appropriate sense of urgency; (2) the staff, though hardworking and dedicated, was more concerned with its police functions than with "a positive approach toward improved recruitment, placement, training, and morale building activities;" and (3) the agency was old, and many of its employees were not sufficiently adaptable as to be able to adjust to new demands.

Although a central personnel agency as proposed was not created, many of the Brownlow Committee recommendations were put into effect, some through legislation and some through executive orders. (The proposal that the Commission be replaced by a new agency, however, met with congressional disapproval.) In 1938, President Roosevelt signed executive orders that laid the groundwork for modernization of the federal personnel system. The orders provided that: (1) the civil service rules be completely revised; (2) the merit system be extended almost to the limits of Presidential authority; (3) the Council of Personnel Administration be reorganized and established as an independent agency; (4) the

Commission "initiate, supervise, and enforce a system as uniform as practicable, for the recruitment, examination, certification, promotion from grade to grade, transfer and reinstatement of employees in the classified civil service." In addition, the Commission was required to establish practical training courses for employees in the classified service, in cooperation with operating departments and establishments, the Office of Education, and public and private institutions of learning.

In 1939, the President established within the White House a liaison office for personnel management, to provide a partial solution to the problem of devoting sufficient executive attention to personnel matters.

Although the Commission's role had been strengthened, these actions served to recognize that it was nevertheless limited. A single central agency below the White House level was yet to be achieved.

THE WAR YEARS: NEW RESPONSIBILITIES AND UNPRECEDENTED PROBLEMS

The next decade was a turbulent period for the Commission, characterized by unprecedented problems, added functions, and official concern over what the Commission's full role should be. By a series of actions, Congress gave the Commission additional functions and responsibilities, some of which extended to both competitive and excepted services.

The Hatch Act, passed in 1939 and amended in 1940, controlled the political activities of federal employees in the competitive service and of state and local government workers in jobs financed in whole or in part by federal funds and it named the Commission as its administrator.

The Ramspeck Act of 1940 required most of the New Deal agencies to be staffed by the merit system. Not only did this end the test of political loyalty as a factor in the filling of thousands of jobs, but it greatly extended the Commission's influence and challenged the Commission with unprecedented responsibility.

The Veteran's Preference Act of 1944 further expanded the Commission's responsibility and authority. Among other things, it assured veterans of both preference in initial employment and retention in the service once employed. A particularly far-reaching feature was the appellate process, which gave veterans the right of appeal to the Civil Service Commission whenever they were removed from the service or reduced in rank or pay.

For the first time, then, the Commission was required to evaluate and pass on the management judgment that entered into an agency personnel action to remove or demote an employee. In assigning this role to the Commission, Congress recognized the Commission as a largely independent agency outside the normal lines of executive authority, which undoubtedly contributed to the Commission's difficulty in maintaining good working relationships with federal managers. Now it was required to second-guess their judgment when they decided to undertake the painful process of firing an employee.

Before the Commission was fully able to adjust to the new and expanded responsibilities given to it by the Ramspeck Act, World War II brought about a completely new set of missions to challenge federal personnel managers. Almost overnight, the problem shifted from one of dealing with surplus jobseekers to one of finding the thousands of skilled people required to man the arsenals, shipyards, and civilian war agencies.

The personnel requirements of the government were great and urgent. Many new agencies were created and headed by top-level executives from private business and industry on loan for the duration of the war. Men of action in the habit of exercising considerable authority in their own spheres of influence, they were not prepared to accept restraints on fundamental acts of management such as employment of personnel, even though officially subject to the civil service rules and regulations. Also, competitive examining procedures, even when applied with prime efficiency, take time, and such time was not always available, so urgent was the need. Therefore, the Commission's position was very sensitive.

The agencies desired relief from controls by the Commission, but the Commission, fearful of the long-range effects of relinquishing control, was reluctant. However, for the duration of the war, almost blanket authority was given to the agencies to recruit within the framework of merit procedures to the extent possible, under a special set of regulations known as "war service regulations." Persons appointed under these regulations did not acquire civil service status. They were given appointments known as "war service indefinite," for the duration of the emergency plus 6 months.

The locus of leadership in personnel matters during and immediately following the war years was not the Civil Service Commission but the Council of Personnel Administration (later named the Federal Personnel Council), of which all agency directors of personnel were ex officio members. Established originally as an independent agency, in 1940 the Council had been placed within the administrative framework of the Commission and its staff had been put on the Commission's payroll. Nevertheless, it continued to function basically as a separate agency, charged with the responsibility of advising both the President and the Commission. Since the Commission's program interests were in many ways limited to the competitive service, an independent status was logical. When President Roosevelt created the Council, he simultaneously assured its independence and prestige by appointing as its chairman the distinguished and scholarly Dr. Frederick M. Davenport, a widely known and highly respected former member of Congress from New York.

Although the Council was only an advisory body, it was not prohibited from initiating advice. Consequently, under

Davenport's leadership it did not hesitate to search out and spotlight matters needing attention. When a problem was identified, a committee was usually appointed to study it and make recommendations. Many present-day personnel policies had their origins in the Council.

Working behind the scenes with the Council and the Commission were the White House Liaison Office for Personnel Management and the Bureau of the Budget. The Bureau, as the President's chief agent for improving management on all fronts throughout government, maintained a small but dynamic staff concentrating on personnel management. It needled and cajoled both the Commission and the federal agencies into modifying policies and procedures. It maintained close contact with the Council; its representatives were on almost all important committees of the Council along with members of the Commission's staff and agency representatives. The Bureau staff was in a particularly strategic position, however, for it also had the function of review, for the President, of any action, regardless of origin, that required executive order or legislation.

The strongest leaders in the field of personnel administration were the professionals who had been brought in to establish the agency personnel offices, and the Council provided the opportunity for their voices to be heard. Many members of the Commission's staff, recruited and trained for its more limited and specific functions, either were not fully conversant with or were uninterested in many of the subjects concerning the agencies. Consequently, the Council became the instrument of change, and the Commission was most frequently in the position of responding to pressures for reform rather than innovating.

The situation was not completely satisfactory to anyone. There was recognition of the obvious need for a single central personnel agency but no clear consensus on how to achieve it. The Commission had by law many responsibilities that must be a part of any central personnel agency; yet it did not enjoy the institutional prestige that would inspire a Chief Executive to place his full faith in it.

History clearly shows that the Commission contributed greatly to the war effort by responding to the needs of the day, and the demands on it were staggering. It had to weigh the sensitive elements of public interest and develop adjustments in system that would serve the needs of the emergency. So successful was this effort that the service was able to grow to more than triple its size in a 4-year period without making the system vulnerable to abuse.

In addition, at the close of the war it handled the almost unbelievably complex task of converting the service to peacetime procedures. It successfully met the challenge of developing a program to apply competitive examining procedures to a quantity and variety of jobs previously unknown, while at the same time protecting the rights of returning veterans and career employees who had been displaced through abolition of wartime agencies.

An anomaly of the period was that the minority member of the Commission—not its president—was the guiding light and recognized leader of the Commission. Though a member of the majority party, Harry B. Mitchell, was designated as the Commission's president, it was Arthur S. Flemming, later Secretary of Health, Education, and Welfare in the Eisenhower Administration, who provided both the internal and the external leadership and who directly and imaginatively guided the development of flexible policies for both wartime staffing and conversion to peacetime operations.

This was not the first time a minority commissioner had played a starring role. In the mid-1930's, Dr. Leonard D. White had made great contributions to the Commission's professionalism and programs. In a much earlier era, Republican Commissioner Theodore Roosevelt had been credited with carrying enough influence to persuade Democratic President Grover Cleveland to remove a Democrat whom Cleveland had appointed to the Commission. However, the actual functioning of the minority commissioner as the agency's head was unique.

In spite of its accomplishments during and immediately following the war, the Commission was still haunted by its reputation of earlier years. Rightly or wrongly, it had been cast in the image of an institution staffed by people who would rather whistle the traffic to a stop than take steps necessary to make it move. Any agency exercising control over the actions of another risks being considered negative when it rejects a proposal or disapproves an action that the other considers desirable. The Commission had been in this position since its inception. Its enforcement role had caused it to pursue a path of some independence and had set it apart from the mainstream of managerial control normally flowing from the office of the Chief Executive. A conflict of attitudes had developed that continues, in part, today. In many instances, the Commission felt that it was dealing with agencies for which ends justified means; in turn, some agencies felt that the Commission was concerned only with means. There is reason to conclude that both attitudes were justified on occasion.

THE STRENGTHENING OF THE COMMISSION

Long-range programs for improving the management of the executive branch of the government, initiated in the 1930's but held in abeyance during the war period, were renewed under the Truman Administration when the President appointed a commission under the chairmanship of former President Herbert Hoover to study its organization. The Hoover Commission, as it was popularly known, made a sweeping investigation of all aspects of federal personnel administration, submitting its report in 1949. The report's first recommendation called for the reorganization of the Civil Service Commission to abolish its position of president and create the new one of chairman and to "vest in its Chairman responsibility for its work." It also recommended that the Commission "place primary emphasis on staff functions rather than upon processing a multitude of personnel transactions."

To explain what was meant by staff functions, the report stated that the Commission's responsibility should be to furnish leadership for personnel administration in government by setting standards for personnel programs in agencies, by post-auditing programs, by applying sanctions whenever standards had not been adhered to, and by considering appeals from employees.

To reinforce its recommendation that the Commission rid itself of operating detail, it proposed the transfer of responsibility for recruiting and examining to the departments and agencies, subject to inspection by the Commission. And, although by no means as critical as the report of the Brownlow Committee of the 1930's had been, it nevertheless found the need for recommending a reorganization.

Many of the Hoover Commission recommendations were adopted. In August, 1949, its first recommendation was accomplished when a reorganization plan by President Truman went into effect. It eliminated the old position of president of the Commission and in its place established the position of chairman, giving him responsibility for the direction of the Commission's operations. This change was more dramatic than may have appeared on the surface. It enabled many operating decisions to be made without suffering the time-consuming process of obtaining a vote of three commissioners. It also established one point of contact for both the White House and the agency heads. The reorganization was perhaps the single most significant step in a long struggle toward the central personnel agency that had been so long sought. (The functions of chairman are described in greater detail in Chapter II.)

In 1951, President Truman took another long step toward strengthening the Commission by appointing Robert Ramspeck as its Chairman. Ramspeck, a former congressman from

Georgia who had served with great distinction as chairman of the House Post Office and Civil Service Committee, brought to the job an excellent background of knowledge of the service and its problems. He occupied the job at a difficult time, during the controversial "McCarthy era" when attention was focused on the loyalty of federal employees. Much of the Commission's time during the period was necessarily spent on making certain that there were adequate procedures for determining the fitness of employees. Scandals uncovered in the Bureau of Internal Revenue required unusual effort by the Commission. Under Ramspeck, procedures were developed for staffing the agency, which contributed greatly to restoration of public confidence in its performance. He also placed the Commission institutionally on record as the defender of the career service and career employee against general or unfounded charges of incompetence and disloyalty.

Although the twenty years of Democratic administration began with what appeared to be a bleak outlook for the merit system and the Commission, they ended in an atmosphere of optimism. The merit system had been extended to 85 per cent of the total government service—a new high—and the Commission had been materially strengthened.

Prestige Under Eisenhower

In 1952, when President Eisenhower took office, the Commission faced a perplexing dilemma. The Administration represented a party that had been out of power for a long time, government service had expanded tremendously, and the merit system had been extended to a point where little patronage was available. Many incoming Republicans felt that the agencies had been staffed in large measure with loyal Democrats who for the most part had been blanketed into their jobs. Consequently, the Republicans seriously questioned whether the bulk of the career staff would be sympathetic with the new administration's policies. In addition, there had been the highly emotional controversy over the extent to which Communists had infiltrated key positions. As a result, two kinds of loyalty were in question: national and party.

The new administration was under heavy pressure to clean house, and efforts to protect incumbents were likely to be viewed with suspicion. At the same time, career employees looked to the Commission for protection. Campaign oratory emanating from both parties about what would happen if and when the Republicans took over had provided them with a widespread feeling of insecurity.

Fortunately for the Commission and the career service, the Eisenhower Administration did not yield to the pressure for wholesale housecleaning; instead, it initiated a series of actions that established the basis for strengthening the Commission and clarifying its role. The White House Liaison Office for Personnel Management was abolished, and the new position of Presidential advisor on personnel management was established. Phillip Young of New York, a former dean of the Graduate School of Business of Columbia University, was appointed to serve in this position as well as that of Chairman of the Civil Service Commission.

The advisor's close relationship with the President inevitably gave added prestige to the Commission chairmanship. Young effectively resisted the clamor from some of his colleagues in the Administration to replace with Republicans many career people they believed to be Democrats. Likewise, his tenacious support of principles of common sense and justice prevented wholesale use of loyalty and security issues to purge the rolls of unwanted personnel. In addition to withstanding the negative forces, he led the Commission staff into a series of positive program activities that gave it prestige it had not previously enjoyed.

The Federal Personnel Council was abolished by Congress in 1953. The function of interagency consultation on personnel matters was assigned to the executive director of the Commission's staff. (See Chapter II for a full discussion of the staff and executive director.) As a vehicle for such consultation, the Commission established the Inter-Agency Advisory Group. Thus, agencies, through their personnel directors who were members of the group, were still given a voice in policy formulation but at the staff level in the Civil Service Commission, not the policy-making level in such an independent body as the Federal Personnel Council.

Another action destined to strengthen the Commission was the appointment of a career employee from another agency as executive director. This responded to the critics who felt that the Commission's staff was inbred and not sufficiently responsive to agency needs.

Shortly thereafter, the staff was reorganized to enable it to assume part of the role formerly played by the White House, the Bureau of the Budget, and the Federal Personnel Council. In 1954, it participated for the first time in the development of a complete legislative program for personnel management in the federal service. The program was submitted to Congress by President Eisenhower, and most of it was enacted into law.

The Commission began to move to other areas to give the answer to those who had earlier criticized it for lack of leadership. In 1955, it marshaled the cooperation of all federal agencies and launched the most extensive program ever undertaken for recruiting in the colleges and universities throughout the country. It also began to broaden its activities in employee training and evaluation of agency personnel-management programs.

In 1957, Young left the Commission to become U.S. Ambassador to the Netherlands, and he was succeeded by Harris D. Ellsworth, former member of Congress from Oregon. Ellsworth's job was different, however, for the consolidation of the duties of the Presidential advisor for personnel management with those of the Chairman of the Civil Service Commission was not to last. In September, 1957, the functions were separated again, and a White House position of special assistant to the President for personnel management was established and filled.

During this period, the Commission's role once more came under scrutiny and was the subject of considerable debate. Some questioned the wisdom of having it under direct White House control, as it had been when Young was Chairman, and felt that involvement of the Chairman in political considerations, inevitably a part of a White House personnel function, brought the merit system into danger. This group generally believed in a Commission almost independent of the Chief Executive.

Others felt that the Commission's exercise of its quasi-judicial functions in handling such matters as appeals was incompatible with service under the President in the conduct of his personnel management functions. This point of view received wide attention when Senator Joseph S. Clark of Pennsylvania introduced a bill to establish an office of personnel management in the Executive Office of the President and transfer to it most of the functions and staff of the Commission. The only functions to be left with the Commission according to the report of the Senate Post Office and Civil Service Committee were "those associated with its watch-dog role as protector of the merit system." The Clark bill received wide support from political scientists and students of public administration, but like its predecessors, it failed to receive the congressional support necessary to become law.

Relatively undisturbed by the discussion surrounding it, the Commission under Ellsworth continued to move, though the pace was different. He provided a conservative leadership, stoutly defending the institution and protecting its gains without looking for new territory to conquer. This course tended to make the members of the staff a little restless. Still feeling the barbs of their critics, and having acquired new prestige and vitality during the first Eisenhower Administration, they were eager for action. Under Young, they had been busily responding to leadership from the top; now they were attempting to push the top into action and were frequently impatient with the rate of progress.

Ellsworth was succeeded in 1959 by Roger W. Jones, who had come up through the career ranks in the Treasury Department and Bureau of the Budget. His knowledge of federal agencies and programs, combined with years of experience at the top executive levels bridging both Republican and Democratic administrations, made him unusually well qualified. In addition, he enjoyed almost universal respect of congressional leaders of both parties. Although Jones's tenure was short, he made lasting contributions. Perhaps one of his greatest was the strong position he took concerning the institutional relationship of the Commission and the White House. He gave effective voice to the belief that the Commission could function only as an arm of the Chief Executive and that this role had been determined by the Civil Service Act, which created the Commission. He argued that it was fallacious to reason that an institution having quasi-judicial functions such as the Commission's appellate activity could not retain sufficient independence to discharge its responsibility under the law and at the same time carry out other activities under direction of the President. His point of view was lucidly and forcefully stated in hearings before the Senate Post Office and Civil Service Committee on the Clark bill and undoubtedly was influential in clearing the air.

A strong believer in the importance of the career staff's being responsive to changes in political leadership, Jones, in 1960, led the Commission and the entire career personnel-management structure in the agencies in an imaginative activity to prepare for the change of administration in 1961. Knowing that there would be change and a period of transition regardless of who won the election, he required the Commission's staff to make plans to assist in an orderly transition, hoping to avoid some of the problems of earlier changes. The exercise was important not only for its value in meeting the immediate problem but for inspiring career personnel-management specialists both to recognize their responsibilities and to acquire the professional competence to carry them out whenever a change in political leadership takes place. Under his leadership the Commission was both aggressive and affirmative, but, because of the separate White House office, its responsibilities were still more narrow than had been envisioned for a single central personnel agency.

THE KENNEDY AND JOHNSON ERAS

The role of the Commission began to grow when John F. Kennedy's Administration took office in 1961, when John W. Macy, Jr., was appointed Chairman. Not only was Macy cut to the mold of the New Frontiersman of the day, a youthful and tireless worker, but he brought remarkable credentials to the job. He had grown up in the competitive service, starting out as an intern upon graduation from college and capping his career with 4 years as executive director of the Commission before temporarily leaving in 1957 to assume the vice-presidency of Wesleyan University.

Almost immediately after Macy assumed the chairmanship, the influence and activities of the Commission were greatly extended. The institution moved in every direction. Matters that it had been content to consider within the domain of agency management became the concern of the Commission's staff. And, again, when the job of presidential advisor was left unfilled, it was clear from the beginning that —although the arrangement was less formal than it had been in the first Eisenhower Administration—the Chairman of the Commission was to play an expanded role.

When Lyndon Johnson became President, any question concerning the location of central personnel leadership during his Administration was erased. He issued an executive order abolishing the position of special assistant to the President for personnel management and, by the simple expedient of addressing a letter to the Chairman, named him his chief personnel advisor:

Dear John:

I have today signed an Executive Order revoking Executive Order 10729 dated September 16, 1957, which established a position of Special Assistant to the President for Personnel Management in the White House.

I shall look to you for advice and leadership on Government-wide problems of civilian personnel policy and management. I am satisfied that this arrangement is a good one and that it should be continued.

Accordingly, and in addition to fulfilling your role as Chairman of the United States Civil Service Commission, I request you to provide advice and assistance to me in all areas of the President's responsibility for civilian personnel at home and abroad.

Sincerely,
LYNDON B. JOHNSON

This formal recognition followed by specific work assignments gave the Commission its greatest stature and also signaled the end of the already declining role of the Bureau of the Budget as a leader in the formulation of personnel policy. The staff of the Commission provided the Chairman with most of the manpower essential to the performance of his added duties. As a result, in 1968, the Commission was carrying out a program and wielding an influence barely resembling that of 2 decades earlier. Though there are agencies such as the Tennessee Valley Authority, the Atomic Energy Commission, and the Foreign Service of the United States that are exempt from the competitive service by law, the fact that the Chairman of the Civil Service Commission was held accountable by the President on all phases of personnel administration automatically brought about an essential coordination and made of the Commission a more dynamic and responsive organization.

Although the manner in which Presidents Eisenhower, Kennedy, and Johnson utilized the Commission contributed immeasurably to its establishment as the central personnel agency, the primary cause has been a composite of congressional attitudes, actions, and inactions. At least one President and a number of political scientists and public-administration students declared themselves in favor of a different approach, but, in the end, Congress denied the authority for a special agency sought by President Roosevelt in the 1930's and failed to enact the Clark bill in the 1950's. Without positive action to establish such an agency, there was a void that had to be filled. No one could deny that, as long as the Commission existed with the functions assigned to it, much of the government personnel job must be done by it. But, more significant than denial of congressional authority to abolish or radically reduce the scope of its activity was the fact that, while experts could study and recommend and students of public administration could debate, Congress continued to assign the Commission more functions.

Such congressional actions have been unsystematic. Although Congress has assigned the Commission specific functions as problems have developed, there has been no act of Congress to define the role of the Commission as the central personnel agency. Many of the functions performed by the Commission in 1968 could be removed from it by Presidential action. Consequently, in the absence of legislation, its future role will depend on how each particular President chooses to operate. If congressional precedent is a criterion, however, any action to weaken the institution will meet with resistance.

Because of the way in which it developed, the Commission today is different things to different people. To the merit-system zealot, it is the only hope for good government—even though its performance is sometimes disappointing, since it does not always appear ready to commit the final act of heroism in defense of principle. To the jobseeker, it is a high blank wall or an open door, depending upon his success at finding the job he wants. To the politician desiring a position for an influential constituent, it is a group of bothersome bureaucrats. To the busy federal executive, it is a required nuisance, welcome when protecting him from the importunities of the unwanted jobseeker but a handicap when preventing an action he wishes to take. To the federal career employee, it is an institution that should be doing a lot more about many things.

II

Inside the Glass Doors

By the close of World War II, many government agencies had given themselves a contemporary appearance by modernizing their offices and equipment. The Civil Service Commission, however, was not among them. As recently as 1955, many of its employees were still sitting on round-backed kitchen-type chairs, working at oak tables scarred from years of service. Although the need for new equipment and facilities was recognized by the commissioners then in office, the parsimonious administration of their predecessors had left a legacy that would require some time to overcome.

Long gone were the green eyeshades and sateen sleeve-protectors that characterized the officeworker of an earlier era, but it required only a little imagination to see them in place as one walked the corridors of the Commission. Not only did the furniture and equipment recall a bygone day, but the Commission was housed in some of Washington's oldest and dingiest buildings. Through lack of either influence with the persons responsible for procurement of office space or proper self-motivation, its quarters were far from first class. All this contributed to an image of obsolescence. The outside observer could be excused for believing that the Commission's staff was incapable of navigating the swift currents that constituted the main channel of public personnel administration of the mid-twentieth century. Thus, the Commission was in a doubly difficult position. It not only had important work to do, but it had to convince a skeptical public of its ability to rise above its environment.

Fortunately, events of recent years have dramatically altered the image. As a result of aggressive work by commissioners and staff, impressions drawn from present physical appearances are the direct opposite of those of two decades ago. In 1963, the agency moved into its first new building at 1900 E Street, N.W., a prestigious location between the Interior and State departments. Designed specifically for the Commission, the seven-story glass and stone structure is typical of modern Washington. It is not lavish, but it compares favorably with the best of the federal office buildings, and, for the first time since World War II, all employees work in one building. A stroll through the corridors gives an impression of a dynamic, modern business organization harmonizing the efforts of people and computers in the production of a vital service to the largest employer in the world.

It is an extremely busy place. Through its front doors come the general public to secure information about job opportunities or to take civil service examinations, while below, in the drive-in rotunda, government limousines wait as an undersecretary of some department confers in the fifth-floor executive offices of the Chairman. In its training rooms, representatives of many federal agencies participate in Commission-sponsored courses on a great number of subjects. In its carpeted conference rooms, Commission and agency representatives discuss problems of mutual concern.

The Commission presents to the public an image of organizational simplicity greater than that viewed from the inside. The internal operations are complex, for, although the three-man Commission is responsible for determining policy, the Chairman is generally responsible for carrying it out, subject only to such review as his fellow commissioners might wish to make. With few exceptions, the staff reports to the Chairman.

This distribution of responsibilities, required by statute, is essentially a compromise with those who would have separated the policy-making and operating functions into different agencies. Although the organizational subtlety that results presents no problem for the public, it occasionally causes a headache for employees of the Commission. So wide are the activities of the staff and so great is the delegation of authority to act that it is sometimes easy to fall into a trap and forget that one is dealing with a matter that affects policy, which only the full three-man Commission can make.

THE COMMISSIONERS

The three commissioners are appointed by the President, with the advice and consent of the Senate, for six-year terms. The terms overlap, one expiring every two years. Not more than two members may be of the same political party. Although not so required by law, the two of one party are usually of the majority party. One term always expires in the first year of a new administration, thus giving the President an opportunity to appoint a person of his own choice and assure a majority shortly after taking office. However, an interesting feature of the law is that, although it provides for term appointments, it also provides that the President may remove a commissioner. An incoming President could, if he wished, vacate all three positions and appoint persons of his own choice.

One of the members of the Commission is named by the President as its Chairman, and another is designated as vice-chairman. Usually, the Chairman and vice-chairman are members of the party in power, although the law does not prevent the President from naming a minority member to either post.

Except for the Chairman, and the vice-chairman in his absence, a commissioner's duties, as provided by law, consist of the things that the three-member Commission must do as a formal body. This is not to say that they may not take on special assignments or engage in such activities as they individually may feel are in the public interest. In general, however, their functions include deciding and reviewing policy, promulgating new rules, recommending legislation, preventing pernicious political activity, considering appeals, and, if they choose, reviewing the Commission's operation after the fact. It is, perhaps, greatly an oversimplification to define their role in such few words, for there are many policy questions constantly before the Commission, most of which are extremely sensitive and important to the efficiency and economy of government operations as well as the welfare of the many federal employees. Many of these questions will be discussed in the ensuing chapters.

The Chairman, in addition to presiding as the head of the Commission, is responsible for carrying out the Commission's policies and generally directing the agency's operations, including appointment of personnel and assignment of work, except for the few activities that the law reserves to the full Commission. The Chairman has recently carried out additional functions that in former days were handled exclusively by members of the White House staff. In the Johnson Administration, he was an important member of the inner circle of the President's official family and, with totally unprecedented activity, directed a program for recruitment of able people for Cabinet offices, headships of independent agencies, commission memberships, and other positions for which the President is the appointing officer. In carrying out this activity, the Chairman maintained a separate office and a small staff in the Executive Office Building. He was also the official administration spokesman on all federal personnel matters.

THE COMMISSION MEETING

Although a primary function of the Commission is to see that federal personnel administration is conducted in an atmosphere free of partisan favoritism, each of the three commissioners retains his political identity. Even the most junior staff member is made aware that two of the commissioners are of one party and one is of the other. The reminders are usually in the form of good-natured banter, however, for there is in reality little opportunity or reason for partisanship. Commission meetings on serious subjects are frequently lightened by friendly needling between the majority and minority members.

The minority commissioner has a unique role. If a matter is to be decided on partisan lines, he can always be out-voted, and thus he wields very little influence. His value lies chiefly in his ability to bring a point of view to bear on policy considerations. Merely the existence of a minority commissioner gives the majority a good barometer. The two commissioners of the majority party are unlikely to take an action that they know is going to meet with organized disapproval of the minority party. Relationships between the commissioners have normally been characterized by a high degree of friendly informality. Not all decisions are unanimous, but the members work together with respect for each other's responsibility. Generally, minority members elect to play on the team but ruggedly resist the things that they feel might favor the party in power.

The commissioners meet not at regularly scheduled times but as frequently as circumstances demand. Their executive assistant arranges the meetings, plans the agendas, and keeps the minutes. Meetings are held in a specially designed, panelled conference room, in the executive suite adjacent to the commissioners' offices, that contains a large tapered table. The three commissioners sit at its head, the Chairman in the center with the vice-chairman on his right and the third commissioner on his left. The executive director occupies the same position to their right. There is no standard arrangement for the seating of other participants at the table. Attendance is restricted to those whose presence is required. Except in the most unusual circumstances, meetings are not public, and, although held occasionally to hear a presentation by an agency or the representatives of an employee organization, meetings are normally in-house affairs attended only by the commissioners and members of the staff involved in the subject under discussion. Meetings are characterized by much give-and-take, sometimes with vigorous debate among staff members, while the commissioners ask questions.

The Chain of Command

Law requires that the staff members who are employed on functions that are reserved to the full Commission must report directly to the Commission. This requirement has been interpreted as referring to the Office of the General Counsel and the Board of Appeals and Review. These two organizational units are small, employing a total of approximately seventy-five people. With the exception of the personal staff of the commissioners—special assistants and secretaries—all the remaining employees, numbering 5,000 or more, and their activities are under full control of the Chairman through the executive director.

The staff of the Commission is headed by the executive director, who is generally responsible to the Chairman for the day-to-day operation of the Commission. The Chairman delegates most of his authority to the executive director, who in turn delegates to the bureau directors in Washington and regional directors in the field.

Responsibility for managing a program or group of related programs is vested as nearly as practicable in one individual, regardless of where the work may be performed. Thus, the director of the Bureau of Inspections, for example, is responsible for the quality of the inspection program nationwide, even though regional directors, reporting to the deputy executive director, oversee most inspections. "Bureaus" carry on the larger activities, while "offices" are smaller organizational entities having significant responsibilities. Of the total

UNITED STATES CIVIL SERVICE COMMISSION

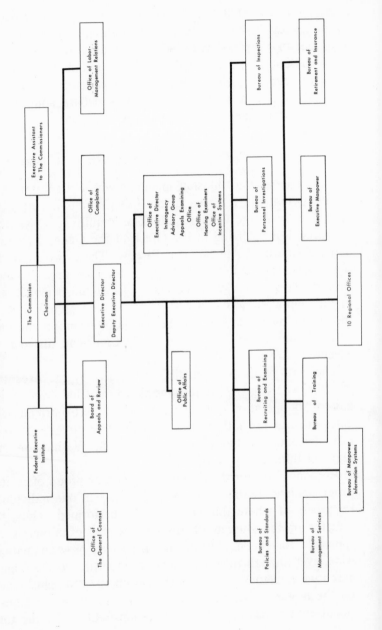

number of employees, approximately 2,000 are in the Washington office; the remaining 3,000 are in the field service.

Bureaus and offices in Washington, in addition to planning and evaluating nationwide programs, must also operate programs for the federal agency in the Washington area. Regional offices are responsible for activities outside Washington. (See Appendix B for the regional boundaries and locations of regional offices.)

The regional offices maintain suboffices in each state at major concentrations of population and federal employment. They are points of contact between the Commission and all agencies or groups concerning any aspect of the Commission's work. Headed by a "Civil Service Representative" and staffed by a secretary, these offices do not do such detailed work as receive applications or provide job information. Rather, their role is to help the federal agencies solve their common problems and to represents the Commission at schools, colleges, and universities as well as civic organizations and others interested in federal employment. The suboffices were established in 1962 to fulfill the widespread public interest in federal personnel matters and to place articulate central-personnel-agency representation close to the employing agencies and the public.

Managing the Work

Extensive authority, under defined program plans and guides, is delegated to bureau, office, and regional directors to conduct the agencies' business within their areas of jurisdiction. Top management has a complex number and variety of activities over which it must maintain control. Therefore, statistical and narrative reports are made systematically and regularly scheduled management conferences are held between the executive director and each bureau or office director. The conferences provide the executive director and his key staff members with opportunity for personal encounter in addition to keeping them attentive to each other's feelings about particular programs and situations. The conferences also serve to prevent "surprises" about the condition of any particular activity.

The conferences are recognized by members of the staff as an excellent management technique, even though they generate a certain amount of natural dread, for the staff must be prepared to answer any question that may occur to the executive director on any aspect of work. Staff members, in turn, conduct similar meetings with key personnel under their direction. The net effect is a management well acquainted with its procedures and problems.

An important instrument in the management of the Commission is its executive staff, made up of the Washington bureau and office directors. The staff is of particular significance in its use as a sounding board and, to some extent, as a review body on government-wide personnel-policy proposals before presentation to the commissioners. The executive director, who chairs the staff, frequently devotes meetings to staff studies of problems and solutions. The opinions of all staff members are sought, even of those having no responsibility in the area under consideration. The meetings are freewheeling with no holds barred, and many a policy proposal has been unable to withstand the buffeting it has taken in the process. It is generally believed that, if a proposal cannot pass the test of the Commission's internal critics, it most surely can expect trouble when it enters the public arena.

During recent years, the Chairman and the commissioners have met biweekly with the staff. The sessions brief the members confidentially on matters that the Chairman has been involved in and that he feels the staff should be aware of, as well as provide informal discussions between the staff and the commissioners on significant items of business. Additionally, these meetings are important because the operational latitude necessarily given the staff enables it to engage in important negotiations and make decisions that do not require advance approval by the commissioners; the sessions, thus, make it possible for them to catch up on news of events in which they have not had a direct hand.

As in any organization in which activities are widely scattered geographically, communication is a problem. The Commission's answer is to err, if err it must, on the side of over-communication; the result is a tremendous flow of paper. The in-box of the staff executive is constantly being filled with copies of material emanating from all offices. The theory is that, if he remains uninformed, it is his own responsibility.

Because of the reporting line to the Chairman, who is responsible for all operations, contacts with him are so frequent and direct that he is rarely uninformed. But, because the two other commissioners are generally not involved in day-to-day operations, there is always the problem called "keeping the two other commissioners informed." For years, the executive director has reminded the staff of their reporting responsibility, and generally their performance has been good. But it occasionally misfires, and something about which the commissioners have never been informed breaks into print or gets circulated in federal personnel channels. There is never any desire or effort to exclude them from information, but, because so much activity necessarily occurs at so fast a pace, courtesy is sometimes forgotten; when it is, the executive director can expect two embarrassing telephone calls, one from each of "the two other commissioners."

DETERMINING POLICY

One of the best illustrations of how the Commission functions internally is seen in the mechanics of formulating personnel policy, which permeates all functions and programs. The Commission's policy role is twofold: not only does it initiate new policy on its own, but it evaluates proposals originating elsewhere. Therefore, it must keep abreast of developments in industry and in state and local government employment jurisdictions. Although proposals are researched by the staff, the final decision for action rests with the commissioners, the President, or Congress, depending on who has authority in the particular instance.

Policy proposals from outside the Commission may originate as bills introduced in Congress or as recommendations from a federal agency, an employee organization, or some other group. When a bill is introduced, it is normally referred to the Commission for its reaction, which represents the official position of the executive branch of the government. The Commission's procedures for evaluating and commenting on bills depend on circumstance. Some bills, for example, result from extensive study and investigation, including public hearings, during which the Commission has already had an opportunity to consider the matter and make its position known. Others are introduced without much advance study, and consideration of them may entail a great deal of work or only the routine submission of brief written comments. From 200 to 400 bills requiring the Commission's attention are normally introduced in each session of Congress.

Policy proposals originating within the executive branch follow a carefully worked out plan. When a problem and the solution proposed requires new or revised policy, the proposal is referred to the Commission's Bureau of Policies and Standards. From this point on, the steps vary with the complexity and sensitivity of the issues. Sometimes urgent time requirements necessitate short cuts. Normally, however, a formal study project is established. If the matter is of special sensitivity, approval of the commissioners is sought before any work is initiated. Ordinarily, an interbureau committee is created to assure that all interested units of the Commission's staff are properly involved. Either simultaneously or subsequently, a committee of the interagency advisory group may be formed to introduce a representative cross-section of agency experience. In any event, many bases have to be touched before a policy is actually adopted.

Any proposed policy that has significant agency interest— there are very few that do not—requires contact with the agencies to obtain their points of view. Even though a committee of agency representatives may have participated in the proposal's development, all agencies must be given an opportunity to react to it. In addition, the views of employee organizations are sought. Unions, even when they have no direct interest, are often asked their advice or kept informed. Outside groups, such as representatives of the academic community, are frequently consulted, for both advice and support.

A policy question may be resolved by merely issuing or adopting an operating program. But, even though such matters are wholly within the authority of the commissioners, the White House as well as representatives of the Senate and House Post Office and Civil Service committees are contacted when unusually sensitive issues are involved. Thus, policy does not happen accidentally.

Even within the Commission, a proposal's route is tortuous. Although the Bureau of Policies and Standards is responsible for the staff's work, every policy proposal must first be cleared through each bureau and office with an interest in it and must be formally presented to the Commission through the executive director. The proposal upon which the Commission acts is usually in the form of a memorandum to which the appropriate staff study is attached. In every instance, the file must show the positions of the various bureaus and offices interested. The Commission encourages complete candor on the part of the staff, so the executive director frequently receives proposals reflecting disagreements.

In most instances when the executive director cannot get agreement, he takes a position, after listening to all arguments, and sends a recommendation to the Commission. Although he himself can reconcile the differing points of view and work out a proposal that has the unanimous support of the staff, he invariably makes certain that the commissioners are aware of whatever differing positions have been taken. Sometimes, when a matter is particularly controversial, he merely recommends that the commissioners meet to discuss the proposal and hear the points of view argued, regardless of his own opinion on the matter. Although the Commission may take formal action without discussion—by the method of each commissioner merely reviewing the file and recording his position—meetings are held on practically all significant policy matters. Some require many meetings to resolve.

THE JOB

The composite of the Commission's present-day activities is complex. The Commission's range of decisions affects individual citizens as well as major personnel-policy issues. Its opinions carry great weight with the President and Congress. The employment policies and practices that result from its deliberations have impact on state and local governments as well as private enterprise.

While there are many operational programs and activities that have been given separate organizational identities within the Commission and that reflect its varied mission, the bulk may be grouped into three basic, or "core," programs. Considered the most basic of all civil service programs, because it was the subject of the original Civil Service Act for which the Commission was created, is the civil service examining function. It is the oldest operating program, but it is still perhaps the most significant to the American public, for it assumes responsibility for the quality of the men and women who fulfill the demanding tasks of civilian government in today's complex society.

A second major program specifically concerns federal employees. This is really a group of programs that involve but are by no means limited to such diverse activities as conduct of training and development programs, design of systems for assuring fair and equitable treatment in promotions, enhancement of opportunities for transfer among agencies, as well as operation of the complex federal retirement system.

The third major area of concern involves enforcement. The size of the federal service and the extent to which authority is delegated to agencies make the assurance of compliance with the federal merit system and related laws and regulations a major Commission function. These three areas of activity are discussed in detail in Chapters III, IV, and V.

As the central personnel agency, the Commission is at the nerve center of the total federal structure. The increasing complexity of society is immediately mirrored in the complexity of government operation. When a new problem is identified, the federal government's answer is a new program. New programs require new people, so the personnel processes must respond.

When public and private employers are called upon to help solve a social problem by using employment to train the economically and educationally disadvantaged, the Commission, representing the largest employer of all, must find the means of assuring that the federal government does its share; more than that, it provides the example of a model employer. Or, if an important segment of the academic community criticizes the procedures for recruiting graduates of their curricula into the federal service, the procedures must be re-examined and defended or modified, as the findings warrant. Whatever the problem, the Commission must try to be completely attentive to the new, while not slighting or sacrificing its historic mission—that of assuring that the federal service is staffed on a merit basis.

III

"From Among Those Graded Highest"

Maternity-garment fitter at an Air Force base in New England and funeral director in Alaska are two extremes of the occupational mixtures comprising the federal civil service. In between is every conceivable type of occupation—doctor, lawyer, engineer, research psychologist, postmaster, business manager, electrician, sheet-metal worker. Whatever the job, it may be found in the federal service and, in all probability, it is subject to a civil service examination. The challenge to the competitive examining system is that it must be adapted to cover every kind of work and almost every kind of working situation.

Most news stories about the federal government are Washington centered, where the civil service is largely white collar and administrative, but almost 90 per cent of all federal employees work outside Washington—many where the action is anything but clerical. The vast majority are within the fifty states, but some are scattered around the world. There are approximately sixty federal executive-branch agencies with civil service personnel, but only three agencies—the Department of Defense, the Post Office Department, and the Veterans Administration—account for 75 per cent of all full-time permanent employment in the executive branch. The types of facilities in which people are employed range from a small post office to a large industrial complex, from a school on an Indian reservation to space-exploration headquarters at Cape Kennedy.

In June, 1967, there were 3,002,461 civilian employees in all branches of government. Of these, 2,485,863 were in the competitive civil service and subject to civil service examining procedures. In the fiscal year ending June 30, 1967, the civil service examining system was called upon to produce more than 500,000 new employees, necessitating the processing of 2,948,583 applications. People were hired to fill vacanies created by both payroll expansion and normal personnel turnover. Largely because of Department of Defense activity related to the Vietnam war, 1967 was a big year. However, new employees taken on through the examining system averaged 375,000 annually from 1962 through 1966.

The number of jobs to be filled, the number of occupations, and the wide geographic dispersal together make the staffing of the federal service a problem of immense proportions. That hiring is accomplished through a system of open competitive examinations complicates the task even more.

The basis for the open competitive examination is the Civil Service Act. The first duty of the commissioners as delineated in it is that of aiding the President by preparing suitable rules for carrying the Act into effect. The Act also specified that the rules should provide, "as nearly as the conditions of good administration will warrant," for open competitive examinations to test the fitness of applicants for public service; that such examinations be practical; that all offices, places, and employments be filled by selection "from among those graded highest"; and that appointments in the departments in Washington be apportioned among the several states and territories and the District of Columbia according to the most recent census.

While these provisions of the 1883 law are the foundation of the civil service examining system, they have, of course, been supplemented by other legislation such as the Veteran's

Preference Act discussed later in the chapter and special requirements set forth in the Commission's annual appropriation. (See Chapters VIII and IX.)

The Civil Service Act has been interpreted as applying to all civilian positions in the executive branch unless Congress enacts specific legislation to the contrary, as it has done with respect to the Federal Bureau of Investigation, the Atomic Energy Commission, and the Tennessee Valley Authority. However, by stating that positions should be filled by open competitive examinations "as nearly as the conditions of good administration will warrant," the provisions of the civil service law recognize that it might not be practicable to fill all positions in that manner. Therefore, the fact that a position is under the purview of the law does not mean that it has to be in the competitive service. It means that someone must make a decision concerning it. The President, through the civil service rules, has delegated to the Commission the authority to determine when a position must be filled by open competitive examinations and when it should be exempt from such requirements and placed in the excepted service. This is one of the Commission's most sensitive responsibilities.

Although the competitive service has been extended almost to the limits of the authority of the executive branch, organizational fluctuations—the establishment of new programs and agencies, and mergers of agencies—cause a continuous flow of recommendations for moving positions in and out of the competitive service. Each year many such recommendations are received from agencies, involving only a single job or a block of jobs.

The Commission faces an agonizing hour when it receives a request to except a position. Each such request challenges the examining system, for, if a decision is made to except the position, there is a risk that the ugly specter of patronage will appear, but, if the Commission rules that competitive procedures still apply, it must guarantee that the procedures can be implemented without undue delay to what may be a vital program. Requests to except positions are normally made by the head of an agency, so the Commission is frequently in the painful position of evaluating the request of a Cabinet officer or some other member of the President's official family. If it denies the request, it risks unhappiness at high levels; if it approves, it must be prepared to defend the decision publicly, for the rules require publication of all such decisions in *The Federal Register.*

No one questions that the competitive-examining procedure restrains a manager's latitude, but there are several additional reasons why agencies might seek relief. Sometimes agencies are in genuine haste to launch a new program or activity that requires new skills and feel that there is no time to pursue the full course of the examining process. Sometimes the motivation for relief is not so pure but is based on political favoritism. It is the Commission's responsibility to assure itself of the true facts in every case and make a decision in the public interest.

The criteria for excepting positions are broad, and there is much room for argument and interpretation. When the Office of Economic Opportunity was organized in 1965, for instance, many of its high-level positions and some of various programs under its general direction were excepted for a two-year period during which competitive-examining procedures were worked out. This exception was allowed even though the Commission had serious misgivings about it. The programs were without precedent, however, and the need to move on them was urgent. Recalling the problems of the New Deal era, when entire agencies were established outside the competitive service, the Commission arrived at the practical solution of requiring the use of existing registers where it was clear that they provided an appropriate means of prompt staffing while permitting exception of positions new to federal employment.

The Peace Corps had earlier made a similar request that the Commission had denied, but Congress later agreed with Director R.. Sargent Shriver and excepted all Peace Corps positions by law, placing them in a special system in some ways like the Foreign Service of the United States.*

The authority to approve the exception of a position is not delegated; a vote of the commissioners is required. Although fault may be found with individual decisions, the over-all statistics tend to support a record of almost continuous expansion of the competitive service. Any ground that has been surrendered has been yielded grudgingly against superior fire power.

Further complicating matters for the Commission is the fact that the principle of filling jobs through civil service examinations has become so widely accepted today that many people endorse and espouse it without really comprehending the complexity of living up to it. Sponsors of the merit system have tended, if not to oversimplify, then to subordinate the problems of administration, so that it has been difficult to draw attention to them lest this action be interpreted as a challenge to the principle itself.

THE CIVIL SERVICE EXAMINATION

To understand the problems of competitive examination, it is necessary first to understand the essential steps in planning, designing, and conducting an examination. First of all, a "qualifications standard" must be prepared—a statement describing the qualities candidates must have to perform a particular job. Each job and group of like jobs is similarly analyzed. The standard must contain no requirements higher that what is essential to do the job, but it must meet certain specifications of law. For example, it cannot specify a maximum age and it cannot require education unless it can be shown that education of a specific type and level is essential

* The regulations affecting the Foreign Service are explained in detail in *The Foreign Service of the United States* by W. Wendell Blancké, a companion volume in the Praeger Library of U.S. Government Departments and Agencies.

to job performance. Only the professions such as medicine and accounting and engineering positions involving research have been allowed educational requirements. For entrance-level positions for which no experience is expected, the standard may simply require a demonstration of the ability to read and write and follow instructions or it may require the demonstration of aptitudes or skills acquired through training, such as typing.

Next, a means of measuring qualifications must be developed, so that the candidates can be ranked competitively. For the jobs of minimum experience requirement, this is done either by a written test of abilities or aptitudes or by a performance test, as in typing. For most jobs above the entrance level, no written test is given; only experience or education, or sometimes both, are evaluated. So that a person who has come prepared with advanced education is not penalized for the time thus spent, four years of education are normally allowed to substitute for three years of experience. Again, the measurement device must allow a means of evaluating the experience of the various candidates in such a way that they can be given relative rankings. Sometimes, however, it is necessary to test aptitudes or skills as well as evaluate experience and education. In these circumstances, the measurement device may include both a written test and an evaluation of experience.

The task of developing tests or other measurement methods that assure that those who pass are capable of performing the job well and that at the same time are simple and economical to administer has challenged the personnel-research specialists since the system began. The law requires that tests be practical, which means that there must be a relationship between the test and the job to be performed. Sometimes it is much easier to determine what to test than how to test it. For instance, in carpentry, skill with tools is important but a particular job may also require ability to read and interpret instructions. For the first part, observation of a candidate's use of tools would be important, but his ability to interpret what he reads must also be tested in some measurable way.

Researchers are constantly seeking improved techniques for all types of examination. In a large municipal civil service jurisdiction, it was once necessary to examine for grooms for the horses of the city's mounted police. Each applicant was given a curry comb and asked to groom a horse while an examiner observed and evaluated his performance. The same horse was used for each applicant, and the examiner soon found that he could learn more by watching the horse instead of the man. If the man knew his business, the horse cooperated; if he did not, the horse nudged him out of the stall. (There is no record of the horse having been put on the city payroll as a civil service examiner. The public likes to believe that civil service examinations are more scientific.)

Sometimes the techniques that the researchers find valid are not publicly acceptable. Because of the large numbers of people to be examined, economy must be emphasized. And, therefore, written tests are heavily relied upon although some jobs clearly require performance-demonstration tests as well. The Commission uses the words "assembled" and "unassembled" to describe its examinations. In an assembled examination, the candidate must take a written test. In an unassembled examination, no written test is involved; the candidate is merely evaluated on the basis of the written data he submits describing his experience.

After the qualification standard and the measurement device have been developed, the geographic area from which applications will be accepted must be determined. For Washington, D.C., jobs, this must automatically include all fifty states and the territories. For field locations, the area depends on the nature and scope of the office or installation in which the job is located. Areas of competition may be a single metropolitan commuting area, an entire state, or several states if the job is in a regional office serving more than one state. The area can be broadened if this is necessary to obtain a sufficient number of candidates. There are many jobs in the field service, particularly in science and engineering, for which examinations are open nationwide.

Next, the examination must be announced within the competition area. A circular containing the qualifications standards and application information is made available to the public. The circular also explains how candidates will be evaluated and it allows sufficient time for the filing of applications. Publication of examination announcements is made by posting them on bulletin boards in post offices and other federal office buildings. In addition, copies are sent to members of Congress as well as to schools, colleges, and other organizations where the information is likely to be brought to the attention of qualified individuals. Press releases are sent to news media. Sometimes, when it is believed that normal publicity will not attract enough candidates, advertising is purchased in newspapers and trade and professional journals. The primary purpose of publicity is to make certain that information about an examination is available to all geographically qualified citizens who may wish to participate.

The procedures for conducting the examinations vary. If an examination involves a written test, it must be scheduled and the applicants must be told when and where to report. The number of examining places varies with the areas of competition. For positions in Washington, a test may be conducted at as many as 1,000 examining points, if there are applicants near them; in other competition areas, a test may be given in only one location.

Scheduling and aranging for a large-scale written test takes time. Sufficient test material must be on hand, and, because it is stored at a central location, the time after the closing date for applications must be sufficient for determining how much test material will be needed and for shipping it to the place of the examination.

If the written test is all that is to be given, the examiners may merely score the papers and announce the results to the competitors. If an evaluation of experience is made, however, the examiners must also review the experience statements submitted by the candidates. Since not only what a person has done, but how well he has done it must be determined, many examinations must be accompanied by work records obtained from former employers and supervisors. Sometimes a simple letter of inquiry is all that is necessary, and sometimes a detailed questionnaire is used. The questionnaires, called "vouchers," are designed to elicit information about that part of a candidate's experience considered most relevant to the job he is applying for.

Until recently, most examinations were independently conducted by Commission-supervised boards of examiners in the various federal agencies, although large-scale nationwide written tests were announced and scored by the Commission's own staff.

The total time for the entire testing process varies, of course, with the complexity of the examination, the area of competition, and the number of competitors. From the date of announcement of a new nationwide examination for Washington, involving a written test, until the list of eligible applicants is available, ninety days will normally have elapsed. This, of course, does not include the planning time preceding the announcement. This time schedule relates only to new examinations, however. Many examinations today are continuously open to application, and written tests are scheduled at regular intervals. In some localities where there is a shortage of qualified candidates in some occupation, tests are given daily at a publicly announced time. In Washington, stenography tests have been given daily for many years. For these "walk-in" examinations, an applicant merely walks in and is examined without advance arrangement. The papers are immediately scored and made available to appointing offices for consideration.

How Jobs Are Filled

The Commission has had to contend with the great public misunderstanding that all jobs are filled by competitive examination and that the Commission provides the public with information about all vacancies. Neither of these assumptions is valid. Most jobs above the entrance level are filled by promotion of the career employees of the agencies in which the vacancies occur, and outsiders are not necessarily informed of the openings.

All jobs in the competitive service must be filled by appointment from an open competitive examination, promotion or transfer of a qualified career employee, or re-instatement of a qualified former career employee. Each agency has the authority to determine which method it will use. If it elects to fill a vacancy by promotion, transfer, or re-instatement, the Commission ordinarily is not contacted unless the job to be filled is one of the relatively few jobs at the executive level. (A special policy that governs appointments to upper-level positions is discussed in Chapter IV.)

After an examination has been completed, the eligible candidates are ranked by score. The resulting list is the civil service register, and there is a separate register for each examination. Although the Civil Service Act, in requiring that appointments be "made from among those graded highest," did not limit first consideration to the top three names, the policy of so doing was early adopted. The "rule of three" was later written into law in the Veterans Preference Act in 1944.

When an agency wishes to fill a job from outside federal career ranks, it requests the name of an applicant from the Commission office that holds the appropriate register. The office examines the request and, in a list sent to the agency called "certificate of eligibles," it certifies the names of eligible candidates. This list must be used to fill the job if an appointment is made from outside the agency, unless the certified candidates are not available or unless the agency can prove to the satisfaction of the Commission that some of the candidates are not qualified for the particular position.

Agencies sometimes have jobs with specialized requirements, as, for example, a secretarial job for which knowledge of a foreign language is essential. If the Commission agrees that such qualification requirements are valid, it limits certification to persons on the register who have the specified background. This is known as "selective certification."

The Veterans Preference Act requires that five or ten points be added to the scores of honorably discharged veterans who pass their examinations. Five points are added to the passing scores of able veterans and ten points to those of disabled veterans. In addition, disabled veterans who receive compensation from the Veterans Administration for 10 per cent or more disability are placed at the top of the registers for nonprofessional positions, regardless of their scores. Thus, three such compensably disabled veterans on a list must be certified before any other applicants. An agency may not appoint a nonveteran from a certificate of eligibles if there is a qualified veteran standing higher on the certificate.

Agencies are required to use certificates or return them unused within a specified number of days. While a name is on certificate to one agency, it is normally not certified to another agency. When an agency reports a selection from a certificate, that name is removed from the register.

The application is a key part of the examining process. Every candidate must complete one at some point, and final eligibility may depend upon its content. In an unasssembled examination, the application may represent the candidate's only opportunity to prove his qualifications. Not only is the application essential to the examiners, but it also accompanies the certificate of eligibles to the employing agency. It provides biographical information and other essentials that enable the appointing officer to make a selection and complete the employment transaction. It is an important element in the federal employment process, and its development involves a relatively unsung but nevertheless significant accomplishment by the Commission.

Many years ago, a form that was used in one of the Commission's examinations contained what seemed to be a clear instruction to applicants to "list all jobs you have held in reverse chronological order." It brought the unexpected response from one applicant that he could not fill out the form since he had never held a job in reverse chronological order. Such experiences taught the Commission planners that great care must be used in phrasing questions to assure that the desired information is obtained. Each form automatically gets a critical review by the many applicants required to fill it out, and they can be expected to direct attention to all errors and injudicious language.

Revision of the basic application form is a solemn and painstaking venture. An excess of 20 million copies are used annually. A revised form was introduced in July, 1968, after a two-year study by a special task force. The initial printing order was for 35 million copies. Therefore, unless some especially sharp-eyed citizen discovers an embarrassing flaw, it will be a familiar sight in employment offices for a long time to come.

In earlier days, the Commission limited its measurement of the candidates' fitness to written tests and applications accompanied by supporting statements submitted by the applicants themselves, with sometimes a supplement derived by inquiries of former employers and references. Late in the 1920's, however, when examining for positions in the Bureau of Prohibition, the Commission realized that sometimes more than this was needed. While tests could measure ability, they did not determine such things as character and reliability. During the latter part of the 1930's and early in the 1940's, the additional question of loyalty to the government had to be answered.

Today, the Commission's investigative program is one of its

largest activities. The Bureau of Personnel Investigations is responsible for a large corps of trained investigators stationed throughout the country who conduct investigations and maintain contact with local law-enforcement agencies and other sources of information about job applicants.

Every appointee to the competitive service is investigated with regard to his suitability and loyalty. Although a responsibility of the Commission, the investigation is not generally a part of the competitive examination. Because of the cost of investigation, only persons who are appointed or given serious consideration for appointment are investigated. Therefore, investigation occurs after selection from certificates of eligibles.

Agencies are required by executive order to determine the sensitivity of each job in relation to its capacity to affect the national security. Most positions (approximately 80 per cent) are nonsensitive. Appointments to these may be made subject to later completion of investigation, but a person who is appointed and later found to be unfit will be dropped from the rolls.

The investigation of applicants for positions considered to be critical to the national security must be completed before the appointment is made. In such circumstances, the depth of investigation depends upon the degree of sensitivity of the job. Jobs of the most critical nature require "full field investigation," in which investigators personally go to the communities where the applicants are known and interview persons who have direct knowledge of their backgrounds. For less sensitive positions, pre-employment investigation consists of a check of police records and other records concerning known subversive organizations, maintained by various investigative bodies. Persons determined to be unsuited for sensitive or critical positions are disqualified for the jobs.

While no investigator or executive will guarantee that the system allows no scoundrels to get in, it is generally agreed, with support from the record of recent years, that the odds against such a happening are high indeed.

ADMINISTRATION OF THE SYSTEM

Operation of the nationwide system of competitive examinations is big business. The budgetary appropriation to the Civil Service Commission for the program for fiscal year 1968 was $18,299,000 covering employment of over 1,900 persons. Not included is the cost of personnel and facilities provided by the Post Office Department. Specially designated employees responsible to the Commission at more than a thousand post offices provide information to the public about examinations, and they monitor written tests. In testimony before the House Appropriations Committee in connection with the appropriation for 1968, the Post Office Department estimated the cost of such services to be $5,554,000. Also not included in the Commission's appropriation is the cost of the time of personnel on agency payrolls who serve occasionally as expert examiners in specific subjects.

Historically, the program has had financial difficulties. Getting sufficient resources has plagued the Commission from its earliest days. When the Civil Service Act was passed, it was clear that the examining procedure would be done through boards of examiners made up of agency personnel rather than personnel on the rolls of the Commission.

From the beginning, the plan had defects, pointed out in sharp detail in 1893 by Commissioner Theodore Roosevelt in a letter to Congressman A. M. Dockeray, Chairman of the Joint Committee of Congress to Inquire into the Laws Organizing the Executive Departments. The Commissioner's letter stated in summary that large backlogs of unrated papers were caused by inadequacies in the workforce. The personnel were not of high quality, and the Commission was not in full control of them.

Although there were many efforts to change the system, it continued with varying degrees of success until the mid-1960's. Until recently, no one had found a satisfactory arrangement for keeping examinations under control of the Commission as the law required and, at the same time, assuring that they properly reflected the needs of the employing agencies.

The job of announcing and conducting examinations had been shunted back and forth between the Commission's staff and the agency boards of examiners. At first, the job was done exclusively by agency personnel on Commission-supervised boards, but, after Commissioner Roosevelt began drawing attention to the supervisory problems, much of the work was transferred to staff on the rolls of the Commission.

Enlargement of the federal government late in the 1930's and through the war years, however, made the job too great for the Commission's staff to handle alone, so the agency boards of examiners again did the work. During the 1940's, the Commission launched a program of decentralization and created new boards until, at one time, more than 800 flourished. (The number had decreased to approximately 700 by early in the 1960's.) Emphasis was on placing work outside the Commission in order to get it done. Since the Commission could not force agencies to work, it required its key employees to engage in a selling program to convince agency personnel that they were willing to do the work. As sales ability varied with individuals, so did the results. Consequently, a crazy-quilt pattern emerged: a hodge-podge of boards with overlapping jurisdictions or gerrymandered boundaries defying explanation to the jobseeking public, Congress, and the employing agencies. Few people were happy about the arrangement.

As a result of an exhaustive study begun in 1962, a totally new plan was developed. Operating by 1966–67, it replaced the 700 examining boards in the separate agencies with sixty-five interagency boards serving all agencies within given geographic areas. The boards consist of top federal officials representing the agencies in the areas served. Each is staffed by employees on the Commission rolls and directed by an executive officer.

The establishment of this nationwide network of interagency boards, each with a separate geographic jurisdiction, has provided the basis for a complete program overhaul. From an almost completely decentralized, largely uncoordinated activity, the program is becoming centrally controlled and coordinated. This is but part of an over-all effort throughout the federal service, initiated at President Kennedy's request. (See Chapter VI.)

Automation has helped make this possible. The computer has allowed the scheduling and rating of written tests in volumes previously impossible. The bogy man to administrators of the program in the past was the flood of applications that might follow announcement of an examination—a possibility particularly fearsome if the examinations are for jobs that require no specialized skills. It was always necessary to control the workload by controlling the intake of applications. This expedient meant that examinations were not always open to all candidates regardless of geographic location, except in categories for which there was an insufficient supply of applications to fill all the vacancies.

Today, operators of the examining program work toward open examinations for all categories of jobs and locations at all times. Then all a person would have to do to receive consideration for a job would be to file an application with an interagency board of examiners covering his area, regardless of where he might wish to work. Efforts are being made to achieve complete uniformity so that the examinations and the rating procedures in effect in New England, for example, will be identical with those in the West.

Wherever it is possible, single nationwide examinations are conducted simultaneously for like jobs in all sections of the country and are supplemented by additional local examinations only when absolutely necessary. One of the best examples of this is the Federal Service Entrance Examination, the FSEE. It is an enormous operation, complex to administer but relatively simple for the applicant and the employing agency. Although open at all times, it is publicized anew each fall at the beginning of the college term. Approximately 1 million copies of the announcement are printed and distributed to all points at which information is made available to the public, including college placement offices. The announcement lists the dates of written tests and the names of the cities where they will be given. It also contains a coupon application that the candidate tears out to apply for permission to take a test. The coupon asks for the name and address of the location at which he wishes to be tested. It must be mailed by a specified day to the Commission's Washington office, where the data are fed into the computer, which has a record of all the locations and seating capacities of the rooms used for examinations. When the number of applications received exceeds the capacity of the regularly used examination room at any location, arrangements are made for additional space. At a specified date before the written test, the computer prints out a notice to the applicant telling him when and where to report for his test. It also prints out instructions to the supervisor of the test storage warehouse, telling him the quantity of test material to ship and where to ship it. Copies of the examinations and answer sheets are then distributed to the examiners in charge at the many points. Written tests are almost always of the multiple-choice type, so an individual booklet and answer sheet is necessary for each competitor. For reasons of security, each copy must be scrupulously accounted for. After the test, all material is mailed back to the test storage center, where the number of test booklets is balanced against the shipping records to make certain that all have been returned. The answer sheets are mailed immediately to the Washington office, where they are scored. The results are then forwarded to the civil service region from which the candidate has applied. When the final rating process has been completed, the candidate's name is placed on lists of eligibles appropriate for the areas of the country in which he wishes to work.

While this degree of coordination has not yet been achieved in all the other examinations, it is well under way. The scope of this one examination is shown by the fact that in 1967, 310,000 persons applied. Of these, 151,000 actually took the test, 64,000 passed, and 15,244 were hired.

RECRUITMENT: THE KEY TO QUALITY STAFFING

The Commission believes that the best way to ensure that the federal service has a top-quality career staff is by continually calling the public's attention to the opportunities and satisfactions to be gained in the many jobs to be performed. Although an announcement of an examination keeps the public informed, it does not by any means assure that the best-qualified candidates will apply, so the Commission reinforces examinations with recruitment. Since World War II, the competition for talent, particularly on college campuses, has been so keen that the government has had to engage in a recruiting effort of enormous proportions to secure enough competitors in examinations to meet the needs of the service.

In support of the Federal Service Entrance Examination, the Commission mounted an extensive promotional campaign. It marshaled the collective resources of the federal agencies in a comprehensive effort to bring the story of federal job opportunities to all the nation's four-year colleges. Each agency was asked to participate in the common program, but it was also encouraged to produce its own recruiting literature and make campus visits to call attention to its own jobs. To provide leadership, the Commission established special recruiting offices in the Bureau of Recruiting and Examining in Washington and in the regional offices.

Although it was treated in a different manner, almost equal

emphasis was placed on recruiting high-school graduates possessing immediately marketable skills but not expecting to go to college. Recognizing the responsibility of encouraging education, however, the Commission's high-school recruiting materials have been carefully leavened with information about the importance of continuing education. More recently, in recognition of the expansion of junior-college programs and the large numbers of technicians being trained for immediate employment, a special examination and related recruitment drive has been launched.

Recruitment has been given very broad outlines by the Commission. When the equal-employment-opportunity program initiated studies to find out why more members of minority groups were not passing examinations, the Commission held discussions with educators to stress curriculum improvement in Negro colleges. Other Commission studies on employment statistics have shown that few women were pursuing college courses that would train them for specific government needs. The statistics were fed back to groups interested in expanding employment opportunities for women.

COMPROMISE WITH PATRONAGE

Many Americans, unfortunately, have a picture of civil service examinations gained from observing an examination for postmaster—a job that, paradoxically, as late as January, 1969, was still being filled through the patronage system. On February 5, 1969, President Nixon announced that he was ending the historic practice of filling the positions of postmaster and rural letter carrier through patronage. He also announced that he would ask Congress to eliminate the requirement that appointments be confirmed by the Senate. Even though successful candidates for postmasterships must pass civil service examinations and, once appointed, can obtain the same tenure rights as any other employee of the career service, appointments at all but the very small fourth-class offices are still, at this writing, covered by the Postmaster Act of 1938, which requires, among other things, that appointments be made by the President with the advice and consent of the Senate. An important requirement of the law is that, to be eligible to become a postmaster, a candidate must have resided within the town or delivery zone of the office for at least one year preceding the announcement of the examination. Until recently, it had been the practice for the candidates to be named by the person controlling the patronage for the area in which the post office is located.

The Post Office Department may elect to fill a postmaster-ship by promotion of a Post Office employee. The employee must then pass a noncompetitive examination administered by the Commission. If it is decided to fill the job with some-one other than a postal employee, however, an open com-petitive examination administered by the Commission must be held. The procedures are generally the same for this as for any other examination. It is publicly announced and the test papers are rated under uniform rating procedures. However, because of politics, intense competition, and community inter-est, ratings are given a closer review than in other examina-tions. In the past, candidates who took the examination gen-erally knew that, to be appointed, they had to receive the political endorsement of the appropriate party officials. This frequently resulted in contests and tactics almost totally inconsistent with the merit principle. Many people believe that well-qualified persons frequently do not make application because they are not members of the political party that controls patronage.

Under the Postmaster Act, when a postmastership becomes vacant, the Postmaster General may appoint an acting post-master for six months without approval of the Commission; this appointment may be extended for a longer period but only with the approval of the Commission. In many instances, the acting postmaster is the person chosen by the local party officials for the permanent appointment, but still he must take the examination. If he has been carefully selected and is well qualified, he may do well in the examination, so that he receives the permanent appointment. But, even so, many people find it difficult to believe that the examination has been fairly administered, suspecting that the outcome was predetermined. If, on the other hand, an acting postmaster fails the examination or does not make a score sufficiently high as to be within reach of certification from the list of eligibles, he is embarrassed and so are his sponsors. Frequently at this point, the examining process is challenged. Attempts are made to have the examination set aside and to have a new examination held or to get the test papers reviewed, with the hope that the favored candidate will receive a higher score. Sometimes allegations are made concerning the character, suitability, or residence qualifications of one or more of the candidates, in an effort to disqualify them. The Commission has found that it must make the most meticulous investigation of each charge. The charges occasionally turn out to be based on fact, but all too frequently they are groundless and represent only a last-ditch delaying tactic.

Although the Commission does not like the postmaster-appointment process and has on numerous occasions recommended that it be freed from the influence of politics, nevertheless it defends its postmaster examining. The public attention to each examination requires that the process be defended. Therefore, sufficient manpower and time is always devoted to making certain that the process is of the highest quality possible within existing policy.

THE CONTINUING DRIVE FOR IMPROVEMENT

The changing nature of American life requires continuing modification of the federal job-filling process, and the Commission, to the extent its resources allow, continually strives to improve the manner in which it conducts its business.

Because of the ever-present need for updating, the program

may be radically different in another decade from what it is today, but only the process will have changed. For instance, while great attention has been devoted in recent years to the system of applying measurement techniques to applicants, many members of the staff feel that greater resources are needed for research into improved methods of testing applicant abilities. The problem of finding the best persons for a complex array of occupations scattered geographically to the far reaches of the federal government's activity will surely remain the same. People will still be required to make judgments about people. And all citizens must be provided equal opportunity to compete for jobs to the fullest extent of their abilities.

IV

Toward a Proud and Lively Career

Let the public service be a proud and lively career. And let every man and woman who works in any area of our national government, in any branch, at any level, be able to say with pride and honor in future years: "I served the United States Government in that hour of our nation's need."

To John W. Macy, Jr., then the newly appointed Chairman of the Civil Service Commission, the words above, spoken by President John F. Kennedy in his first State of the Union Message, were both challenge and charter. Much had been done in the Truman and Eisenhower administrations to strengthen the career service and clarify the Commission's responsibilities for its welfare, but this was only a forerunner of things to come.

Macy's personal commitment to improving the public service, combined with presidential interest and backing, meshed well with pressures for change from unions, congressional leaders, academicians, organizations, and individuals. His seemingly inexhaustible energy and almost limitless breadth of interest soon had staff members panting in their efforts to keep up to his pace. His use of the dictating machine outside the normal workday hours—the staff referred to it as "the iron maiden"—produced a continuous stream of memos asking questions and making suggestions. Brief and terse, they were nonetheless important, for he maintained a good follow-up system. They all required response, some with a brief reply but others involving painful, soul-searching studies.

The result was a change of nearly revolutionary proportions in the Commission's attitudes and activities as well as in the structure of the career service itself. Almost every aspect of personnel policy was re-examined. In some instances, entirely new programs were launched. Others already begun were reviewed and extended or modified to provide the conditions in which "proud and lively" service could flourish.

Labor-Management "Consultation"

One of the early, far-reaching actions of the period was President Kennedy's executive order in 1962 recognizing the place of unions in the general fabric of federal personnel management. Union-management relations are somewhat more complex in the federal service than they are in private industry. Since much of what employees normally bargain for —salaries, hours of work, sick leave, vacation time—is fixed by law, there is little opportunity for bargaining or negotiation in the usual sense between labor and management. Also, federal employees do not have the right to strike. Communication between labor and management therefore takes the form of consultation rather than traditional bargaining.

There are, however, many areas in which federal agencies establish specific policies of great concern to employees. The Commission makes changes in government-wide personnel policy within its authority and recommends changes that may be made by the President. It also recommends legislation where there is no authority for a desired action. In all these areas, employee views are important.

Although unions have existed for many years, until the executive order was issued there was no specific charter or set of rules under which they operated in the federal service, other than a stated policy permitting employees to join or refrain from joining as they chose. The objective of the order was to provide machinery for ensuring that unions would have full opportunity to be heard on matters of concern to them. It still permitted employees to join or not as they saw fit, but now it also specified criteria under which unions would be recognized and consulted. It left official recognition of specific unions to the separate agency managements. Although the Commission's initial role was to assist in implementing the order and in evaluating its effectiveness, this role gradually shifted to one of primary responsibility for seeing that federal policy was carried out.

In addition to giving the Commission the added job of developing a proper environment for good union-management relations throughout the service, the new status accorded the unions also changed the Commission's way of doing business. Formerly it had consulted selected leaders of employee organizations on personnel policy matters of concern to them; now it consults the unions on practically every new policy, program, and activity.

BALANCING PAY SCALES

In another activity spearheaded by the Commission, the federal pay system was so completely overhauled that the total career service was shaken until its cornerstones rattled; it suffered an alteration of one of the articles of faith on which recruiting programs had rested.

Under the old system, Congress laboriously set the pay scale for the various job grades after sufficient pressure for action had been generated by the interested parties; the results were not always consistent or businesslike. Because of salary ceilings on top-level jobs, including those of the members of Congress themselves, a general imbalance had occurred. Lower-grade salaries had been pushed up until there was no longer a normal spread from low to high, creating thereby insufficient incentive to join the career service. In an imaginative effort, procedures were approved and developed by Congress for relating federal pay scales to scales in private industry.

It had previously been taken for granted that positions in the public service—at least those at middle and upper levels —could not be expected to pay as much as comparable positions in private enterprise. Federal recruiters had been schooled in the practice of luring people to the service by the attractions of interesting and challenging work rather than financial reward. Now they are able to offer exciting work assignments as well as pay opportunity generally comparable to private industry.

Although pay reform originated in the executive branch and was directed by the Commission, what finally evolved was a composite reflecting the views of the executive, legislative, and judiciary branches along with those of employee organizations. Perhaps the most significant reform was that, for the first time, a system had been adopted for periodic review and adjustment of pay for top federal executives and members of Congress and the judiciary.

In the past, Congress had had to wrestle with the politically distasteful task of setting its own salaries as well as the salaries of top executives. Now, a special commission makes a quadrennial review and determines new rates. The action is subject to congressional veto. If Congress does not act within thirty days, however, the recommendations of the special commission become law. The planned periodic review of top pay levels sets the stage for adoption of a more orderly system for the many jobs at lower levels.

Wholesale revision of the procedures for setting wages for the thousands of blue-collar occupations was then made. Wages for industrial workers had been fixed by the separate federal agencies, which took local prevailing rates as their guide. Consequently, there were widespread discrepancies and inequities. The Commission had long recognized the situation but was powerless to do anything about it. Authority was given by law directly to the agencies. President Johnson solved the problem by using his executive power to require the agencies to coordinate their action under Commission leadership.

THE MERIT SYSTEM AND PROMOTIONS

Since most vacancies above the entrance level are filled by promotion from within the agency with the vacancy, the method by which promotions are made is of utmost importance to employees and the management. Developing a fair and equitable system satisfactory to both has presented problems of unusual difficulty, problems that have harassed the Commission for years.

There is little disagreement with the principle of filling jobs by promotion. Most people agree that it is fair to give the better jobs to persons with experience in the particular activity. However, there is no such unanimity of thought as to how the agency should select the employee to be promoted. Opinions range from those of some appointing officers who desire as much latitude as possible in selection to those of some employees who would like to see management's choice restricted to the top name on a list produced by some completely objective system. In between are all shades of opinion. Some feel that seniority should govern: a job should go to the person next in line with the longest service. Most managers, agreeing that this may be fair to all employees, nevertheless believe that it does not necessarily produce the best qualified. Others recommend that a written examination should be the sole criterion for advancement in some jobs, frequently without realizing that development of a truly valid written examination for some specific purposes may be extremely difficult and expensive, if not impossible.

In earlier years, the Commission kept its hand in the promotion process by requiring that each recommendation be sent to it for approval in advance. When the government became so large during World War II, the Commission was forced to delegate authority for action to the agencies, but it still required that a record of each promotion be forwarded to it for post-audit review. Subsequently, the volume of personnel business forced it to abandon review of each action and substitute a sampling of actions during its agency inspections. Thereafter, it left promotion decisions to the agencies as long as they did not base their actions on such improperly discriminatory reasons as race, religion, or politics. It confined its interest largely to assuring that persons promoted would meet minimum qualifications standards.

Some agencies found it advantageous to introduce merit systems for making promotions; many did not. The absence of a merit system in most agencies, however, led to widespread dissatisfaction. Employees felt that, even though promotions were not made through political patronage, there was a thing called personal patronage that was just as bad. They felt that promotions were going to the friends of the person who had authority to make selections.

The Commission's attitude in the situation was very interesting. Although it was a crusader for the application of merit procedures to initial appointments to the service, it kept its hands off the promotions problem until it was forced to act. Finally, the clamor had become so loud and the voice of the employee leaders had grown so strong and articulate that it was evident that Congress would soon enact legislation. To head off what it feared would be something worse, in 1958, the Commission issued regulations effective January, 1959, requiring each agency to have a merit system for making promotions. The regulations did not specify what the system should be but set forth criteria that it should meet. They still gave the agency much latitude in determining procedure. Agencies were required, however, to maintain records so that inspectors could review their promotion plans.

Although the initial regulations were a necessary first step, employee organizations continued to press for tighter controls. In 1968, after a thorough review and without any trace of its earlier reluctance to move into the promotion field, the Commission materially tightened the regulations.

The Commission still pursues a middle course, however. Some unions would like to see great weight given to seniority and little or none to a supervisor's appraisal of an employee and his work. The Commission has taken the position that supervisory appraisals are important and that seniority should be a deciding factor only when other things are equal. While supporting agency management in this, the Commission held against it by eliminating its long-standing authority to impose written tests even when not required by the Commission.

STAFFING THE HIGHER CAREER LEVELS

No less difficult for the Commission to solve than the problem of establishing a satisfactory merit promotion system for lower-grade jobs was that of developing an adequate plan for filling the top-level jobs, in the $25,000 to $33,000 annual salary range. There are many different kinds of jobs established under a number of different laws. Some laws directly authorize specific agencies to originate and fix the rates of pay for limited numbers of executive jobs in designated activities. The majority of such positions, however, may be established only with the approval of the Commission. Some jobs must be filled by highly specialized research scientists; others require capable administrators who can direct field programs of unusual political sensitivity. For some jobs it is difficult to find qualified personnel; for others, there may be many who are qualified. The latter is most likely to be true when general administrative ability and experience are the prerequisites, rather than professional or technical training.

Regardless of the occupational subject, all jobs are important to the American taxpayer. How well the incumbents perform may determine the nation's advance in science or whether a program of social significance achieves its objectives. The fulfillment of a job has much to say about how well government serves the people.

A relatively quiet controversy over how to improve job-filling procedures took place over a period of many years. That it was quiet was due to the fact that it was largely an in-house matter. The parties to it were, for the most part, students of public administration, federal administrators, personnel managers, the Commission's staff, and a few members of Congress. The general public demonstrated little concern, even while the Hoover Commission made it the subject of a special set of recommendations. The participants in the discussions and studies were generally in agreement that certain jobs were unique and should be the subject of specialized treatment, but there the agreement ended.

The principal recruiting source for most of the jobs was the service itself. The logic and desirability of such practice was normally not challenged. There was widespread feeling, however, that the system did not ensure selection of the best-qualified candidates and that programs were inadequate for developing the experience needed for full performance by persons promoted. Furthermore, there was the belief that the practice of almost always promoting from within an agency led to a kind of bureaucratic inbreeding that made the service unresponsive to new ideas and change. Responsiveness is particularly important during a transition to a new Administration, which must rely upon the top career executives to achieve many of its program goals. Unless these executives can demonstrate competence and loyalty, the service is in jeopardy, for incoming administrations naturally want the greatest possible latitude in filling and vacating positions.

Through the years, as the problem of how best to fill jobs was discussed, many ideas were put forth, including that of a separate service for career executives under its own tenure regulations. No one was able to arrive at an acceptable solution until finally, in 1967, a new plan called the Executive

Assignment System was established by executive order and placed in operation.

In 1963, Chairman Macy had established a study group within the Commission to review the problem in its entirety and develop a program. The effort was given a great boost when President Johnson interested himself in agency selection of top career personnel, and, in an unprecedented action, required candidates to come to the White House for a congratulatory interview before the Commission announced its approval of appointments to the agencies. This action at first caused considerable consternation among skeptical Commission staff members and personnel directors, who automatically assumed it to be an intrusion of political considerations into the selection process. Their fears were quieted, or at least held in check, by assurances that it was merely a demonstration of the importance the President attached to career executives and the processes by which they were selected.

The natural follow-up to this expression of presidential interest was the conclusion that, if it were a matter important enough for White House consideration, it was important enough for the attention of the highest management levels of departments and agencies, As a consequence, the Commission required that each such recommendation be accompanied by a letter from the head of the department or agency certifying that the case had been personally reviewed by him and had his full endorsement.

When the Commission's study group proposed the Executive Assignment System, therefore, drastically modifying the process and restricting the latitude of agency managers, the climate for acceptance was favorable. The plan's foundation is a completely computerized profile of all the 26,000 employees at the executive levels and the next grade below. An agency formerly selected a person it wished to promote and the Commission reviewed the candidate's qualifications against the standards for the job. If he met them, even barely, he was approved. Now, when an agency wishes to fill a job by promotion, it must advise the Commission first. The Commission then refers names and backgrounds of qualified federal government employees from the inventory to the agency, which must consider these names together with its own qualified employees. Then it makes a selection and recommends its appointment to the Commission, making known its specific reasons. If the Commission disapproves of the selection, it cannot require the agency to appoint someone on its qualified list. But the agency must appoint someone the Commission will approve or leave the job unfilled.

In the relatively rare instances in which the agency chooses to appoint from outside the service, it must recruit according to a plan specifically approved for the job in question. The candidates identified through the agency's recruiting effort, along with those whose names are referred by the Commission, must be evaluated and ranked by a board consisting of the top officials of the agency. The results of the evaluation are submitted to the Commission, along with the recruiting plan, specifying which candidate the agency wishes to hire. If the Commission agrees with the recruiting plan and the rankings made by the agency officials, the selection is approved and the person is appointed, acquiring career tenure. (The ranking procedure is not required for science and engineering jobs. The supply of candidates is so inadequate that the competitive principle is not pertinent.) Since the plan is new and without precedent, modifications will no doubt be made. Its success may well be measured by the way in which it is viewed by an incoming administration.

As a companion to tightened selection policies, the Commission also introduced a periodic review of the entire executive-manpower plan of each agency, in order to improve the executive jobs authorized by Congress as well as the personnel assigned to them. In addition, it has moved to strengthen its program of training and development of executives.

INTERAGENCY CAREER OPPORTUNITIES

In seeking a transfer to another federal agency, Mr.——— may apply to the personnel officials of the federal agency in which he would like to work. In filling any position vacancy, the power of appointment rests by law with the agency. His prospects of obtaining a transfer will depend mainly upon his own efforts in interesting the personnel officials in taking the necessary action to effect his noncompetitive appointment. A leaflet which explains the transfer privilege is enclosed.

.   .   .   .

The Commission's main function in transfer actions, so far as other agencies are concerned, is to prescribe the requirements to be met and in certain cases, at the request of the employing agency, to determine whether the person being considered meets those requirements.

The sentences above are from a standard letter the Commission uses in response to requests for assistance from a federal employee seeking a transfer to another agency. It reflects the Commission's traditional position, which circumstances are forcing it to change to the extent that it can.

For many years, its employment information activities were oriented toward providing facts about civil service examinations but not about specific job vacancies. However, federal employees are greatly interested in job openings in agencies other than those they are currently employed in. Responding to this interest without impairing the efficiency of the service has presented a nagging problem to the Commission in recent years.

Although many employees transfer between agencies, the fact that the activity is unsystematized has brought continuous pressure for change. And, although the problem exists in other sections of the country as well, it is particularly acute in the Washington metropole of more than 250,000 federal workers. When the Washington newspapers print the story of a new program or a new office, the telephone circuits to the Commission's job-information center immediately become clogged. The great concentration of employees, all within the same commuting area, reading the same newspapers, and using the same telephone exchange, means a huge volume of calls to the Commission, even when only a small percentage of the area's workers is interested.

The federal government is, of course, the dominant employer in Washington, and persons who desire to advance as rapidly as possible in interesting work, find that their chances lie largely in movement within the government. Even though each agency is a separate employing entity, the government is looked upon as a single employer, and employees naturally expect a central information point concerning job openings.

The Commission recognizes the logical interest of the employees. It believes that a certain amount of movement between agencies is good for the service and that it is important that employees feel they are considered under a fair and impartial system for job openings, wherever they may be. At the same time, the Commission believes that it is important for agencies to have as much latitude as possible for first consideration of their own employees.

The Commission faces a true dilemma. Whenever the problem has been reviewed, the commissioners have concluded that there should be a means of bringing well-qualified career employees to the attention of agencies when the agencies desire to fill a vacancy by transfering an employee from another agency or when they wish to place their own employees in competition with the best available. But at this point, they have always been whipped by logistics.

The Commission has always lacked adequate staff to develop and operate a referral system involving comprehensive placement assistance. Even more important, however, is the tremendous size and complexity of the federal establishment.

Because of the size of many of the individual agencies and the necessity of delegating employing authority to subordinate organizational levels, there are actually more than 350 agency personnel offices within the Washington area alone.

Over the years, there has been considerable experimentation with placement rosters—lists of qualified career employees identified by specialization and referred to agencies with jobs to fill. Most of them have not been successful, however, because problems of compiling them and keeping them up to date have been insurmountable. Activities currently under way offer hope that a solution may be in the offing. The installation of the Executive Assignment System and the Executive Inventory appear to have taken care of the situation at the upper levels.

Recent advances in data-processing may make possible a referral system for the lower levels, although the number of jobs involved is many times larger. The Commission's staff has studied plans for nation-wide rosters in certain categories of federal jobs at the middle levels as a pilot project. If successful, it could be extended to many categories. Thus far, however, lack of funds has held the project back as merely a plan.

The Commission has taken an interim step that is proving helpful. Each of its interagency boards of civil service examiners is located at a large concentration of federal employees, and attached to each board is a job-information center. Agencies are now requested to list with the center any vacancies for which they will consider career employees from other agencies. The plan is ultimately to have each job-information center offer career counseling to employees who desire it.

A system fully responsive to the desires of career employees and the needs of agency management is still some distance away, but present indications are that it will be achieved at least to some degree within the next few years.

CAREER EMPLOYEES OUT OF WORK

Because of the size of the federal service and the fact that programs are constantly changing, there are personnel fluctuations that sometimes reduce a program in size or eliminate it entirely. New programs are established and old ones are enlarged, requiring new personnel. Some agencies may have surpluses of personnel and reduce their workforce while others are recruiting. Normally, such changes grow out of congressional actions on appropriations. They may also result from organizational changes within an agency. The net effect is that each year there are dislocations of career people, some of them with long years of tenure.

The Commission operates a positive program of assistance for the career employee separated from his job through no fault of his own. Its foundation is the carefully worked out and detailed procedure that the agencies must carry out in reducing staff to assure that the tenure rights of career employees are fully protected. When a career employee is separated as a result of a reduction in force, he may file an application with the Commission and be considered for a suitable opening before the list of eligibles is certified. This step prohibits employing anyone from outside the service in jobs for which a displaced career employee is qualified, in the geographical areas in which he wishes consideration, for one year, unless he is reappointed sooner.

Invoking the separated-career-employee procedure is an unhappy process for everyone, particularly the Commission. It restricts the latitude of the agency wanting to fill a vacancy. From the standpoint of the employee out of work, it is not sufficiently positive and takes too long. The Commission cannot demand that anyone hire him; it can only prevent the hiring of anyone else from outside the service.

In the past, agencies have tended to view displaced employees as undesirables and have tried to evade placing them. This has a certain historic validity, for, before reduction-in-force procedures were policed as tightly as they are today, some imaginative personnel officers were accused of such artistic manipulation that only their least-wanted employees were released.

More recently, as the Commission has grown in stature and influence, it has moved forcefully to control reduction separations before they create crises by joining the agency contemplating a reduction in force with other agencies that are hiring, so that they can work out a voluntary placement program. When the Commission moves, it uses a heavy hand and quarterbacks the entire game, making certain that the retrenching agency plays fair in determining whom it releases while applying the same firm hand to the agencies with the capacity to hire. This approach usually makes everyone happier. The employing agency feels that it recognizes the problems of the retrenching agency while having a say about whom it employs. And the employee does not have to wait for a new job or go on the unemployment rolls.

On the whole this cooperative approach has been successful, but it does not always work, for sometimes the qualifications of persons being separated do not match the vacancies. The only thing to do then is to share knowledge of future vacancies to assure consideration of the employee who is off the rolls. Although career employees sometimes suffer from the closing of an office and are out of work for some time, they have generally been able to continue their careers with only minimal interruption.

EMPLOYEE TRAINING

From the little red schoolhouse with a part-time teacher to a university with a full-time faculty in a decade might describe the development of the Commission's employee-training activity. While there has long been employee training of some

THEN

and

This pre-1883 cartoon in *Harper's Weekly* is entitled "The Office-Seekers' Invasion of the White House—Awaiting an Interview with the President."

NOW

Job-seekers at Civil Service Commission headquarters in Washington, D.C., inquire about vacancies and examinations.

From 1932 until 1961, the Civil Service Commission was housed in the old Patent Office, a building recently renovated for the Smithsonian Institution's National Portrait Gallery.

At various times, Commission employees also worked in the venerable Pension Office, now being restored.

Today, the Commission's home is at 1900 E Street, N.W., Washington, D.C.

A typing examination is administered at the Commission's headquarters.

A general written test is taken at the Commission's headquarters.

A Commission representative visits a college campus.

Shown in the Commission's computer room are (left to right) Nicholas J. Oganovic, Executive Director; John E. Beckman, Chief of the Operations Support Division, Bureau of Recruiting and Examining; David S. Williams, Director, Bureau of Management Services; and the author.

There are civil service employees
throughout the U.S. Government...

at the Department of Justice

working for the Office of Economic Opportunity

surveying for the District of Columbia

boarding a vessel in Baltimore harbor for the Bureau of Customs

planning for the Bureau of the Budget

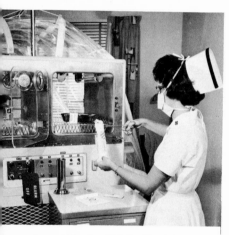

on duty with the Public Health Service at the National Institutes of Health

working with refugees for the Agency for International Development in Vietnam

supervising school lunches for the Department of Agriculture

Vice-Chairman Ludwig J. Andolsek (left) and Commissioner Robert E. Hampton (right), newly appointed Chairman, confer with then Chairman John W. Macy, Jr., on a policy matter.

Dr. Frank Sherwood, director of the newly established Federal Executive Institute in Charlottesville, Virginia, addresses an audience of selected federal executives attending an eight-week session of seminars designed to improve their management techniques.

kind in the federal service, the last ten years have been so action-packed that they must be reviewed briefly to give perspective to the present.

Almost every employer has recognized the responsibility of giving some training to his employees, if only to show them how the cash register works or to explain the mysteries of particular bookkeeping methods. Until comparatively recently, however, training was usually limited to such pragmatic matters as office procedures or the techniques of operating a new machine. For many years, there was little concern in the federal service about training in other areas. With the tremendous expansion of government in the 1930's and 1940's, however, came the realization that the knowledge of employees must be continually updated as science and technology advance and as the demands of society become more complex.

Although no one questioned the propriety—even the necessity—of an agency teaching its own procedures, there was considerable question about more intangible subjects that could be obtained only at a college or a university. Teaching these seemed to conflict with the tradition of expecting a person to pay for his own education beyond high school; conservatives viewed employee education with little enthusiasm. Also considered questionable were supervisory and managerial training, although private industry had seen the economics of providing employees with management techniques that would prepare them for more responsibility. Some agencies, with the more glamorous scientific programs, had sold Congress on the need to pay for employees' college courses, but the practice was far from universal, and some agencies had no authority of any type. The result was a hodge-podge of policy.

The Commission's role was extremely limited. It encouraged agencies in their educational programs but had neither the personnel nor the authority to do more than exhort or make pious pronouncements. Its only direct operation was a management-intern course and two- or three-day sessions held occasionally to meet some specific need in personnel management. Some agencies had training operations that far outstripped those of the Commission.

Change was in the wind, however, for the years of study and concern expressed by the Commission, agency representatives, students of public administration, and congressional leaders resulted in the passage of the Government Employees Training Act in 1958. Sponsored by the House Post Office and Civil Service Committee, the Act provided for a broad, rapidly developing activity in which all federal agencies can participate, under Commission leadership. Its objective was to improve efficiency and keep employees abreast of scientific and management developments. Essential training may be done within government and nongovernmental institutions. Basic-skills education is not authorized unless qualified persons cannot be found for specific jobs. The Commission's role under the Act is both regulatory and operational. It issues regulations for and evaluates the agency training activities and it gives agencies professional advice. In addition, it directly conducts training courses for the agencies.

Developments under the Training Act have been spectacular. The Commission, prior to the Act. had seen the need to educate personnel and had wanted to do so, but it had no funds with which to begin a program. With the Act, it still had no funds, but the law now allowed the agencies to reimburse each other for the cost of employee participation in training courses. Commission officials saw an almost unlimited opportunity for expansion. Seizing a key feature of the Act, which provided that agencies should pool resources to avoid costly duplication of effort, the Commission first printed a catalogue of all courses now open to employees in all agencies. It also began to offer courses financed by fees charged to the agencies. Today, it spends approximately $3 million annually on training, most of which is reimbursed by the agencies.

This by no means reflects the over-all federal employee training endeavor, however. A June, 1967, report of the

Manpower and Civil Service Subcommittee of the House Post Office and Civil Service Committee estimated that by the end of fiscal year 1966 agencies were spending $180 million a year on training, and they expected continued increase. Although the report did not make a judgment on the total amount spent, it put a finger on a vulnerable spot in the Commission's activity. It criticized the Commission for not being sufficiently aggressive in evaluating agency programs or offering advice and assistance and it pointed out that the Training Act called for a pooling of agency resources.

The Commission recognized the validity of the criticism. At the time that the Act was passed, the Commission, believing that training was good, had "accentuated the positive" and encouraged everybody to do likewise. There was little of the negative in its approach for very good reason. Although the law made the Commission responsible for evaluating training activities, fulfillment of this responsibility was hindered by conservative appropriation. About the only money in the cash drawer was what the Commission could eke out of its regular appropriation for its own training courses and what it could collect from agencies for conducting them. Although it did not blush about charging the agencies for employee participation, it somehow could not bring itself to charge them for inspecting their operations.

Agency programs range widely. Some send promising employees to graduate school. Arrangements have been made with colleges and universities near some federal installations to teach courses, usually on federal premises after regular working hours. There is no general requirement, however, that, if a course is considered necessary, it be taken on an employee's own time.

The Commission's program extends throughout the country and has more than 200 employees. They are for the most part organizers, planners, and negotiators. In addition, visiting lecturers number in the thousands. The size of the activity is reflected by the fact that, in fiscal year 1967, 36,430 employees participated in the courses, which ranged from federal economic and social programs to communications and office skills.

The most dramatic development has been the establishment of separate institutions for courses away from the job. Executive seminar centers have been established at Kings Point, New York, and Berkeley, California, where, for a two-to-four-week period, middle-level executives live on campus, attend lectures, and participate in discussions designed to enchance their administrative abilities. The program's brochure states that the objective is to reach executives "from all departments and agencies at that point in their careers when attained or potential positions and responsibility dictate that they expand their views, attitudes, and understanding beyond agency and functional boundaries." The centers are extremely popular with the federal agencies, and they underwrite their cost by reserving a number of spaces each year in advance.

The Commission plans and operates the centers, but there is a close tie to the agencies. A select committee of agency directors of personnel periodically reviews the activity and advises the Commission on program content and all other aspects of the operation.

Another innovation was the establishment in 1968 of the Federal Executive Institute at Charlottesville, Virginia. It culminated a decade of study and discussion by persons in and out of government concerned with improving the management of the government's personnel programs. Patterned somewhat after the concept of the military staff college for senior officers, the purpose of the Institute as stated by the Commission is "to increase the ability of higher civil servants to fulfill their role of providing continuity and responsiveness in the administration of national policies and programs."

The plan of the Institute envisions eight-week classes of thirty executives in residence, participating in a broad curriculum. The course is designed to enhance their ability to lead programs in the agencies that employ them as well as to groom them for more important assignments, perhaps in other agencies.

The Chairman of the Civil Service Commission is directly responsible for the operations of the Institute. Assisting him is an advisory board of nine members appointed by the President for two-year terms. Three of the members are heads of departments or agencies of the executive branch, three are prominent educators, and three represent the public. Thus, with the inauguration of the Institute, the Commission is responsible for a training endeavor reaching all levels of the service. Now, in addition to its own operation, it is trying to strengthen its assistance to agencies and evaluation of their programs, as it gains increases in its own appropriations.

FRINGE BENEFITS

In recent years, the Commission has become increasingly involved in assessing the position of federal employees relative to that of employees of other organizations. It has been continuously concerned with what is pertinent to employee satisfaction and welfare other than salary or compensation.

As Chapter VI will show, the Commission believes that the government should be a model employer. Frequently, however, since many government-wide personnel policies require legislation, and enacting programs into law is usually slow at best, the government lags somewhat behind private industry.

The Commission's posture on liberalization of benefits is generally conservative though modern. The unions have frequently criticized it for being too much oriented toward management—inclined to consider cost rather than employee welfare. The Commission is in a tough position. Because of the number of federal employees, any action enlarging benefits is extremely expensive. An additional cost of one dollar per employee annually adds more than $3 million to the federal budget. Proposals that the work week be reduced from forty to thirty-five hours, for example, have been resisted by the Commission on the grounds that the five-day forty-hour week has not been shown to place an unreasonable demand on an employee's productive capacity and the additional burden to the taxpayers would be enormous.

In spite of the conservatism credited to the Commission, there has been a steady trend toward liberalizing employee benefit programs, and it is generally considered that on the whole the federal employee is taken care of as well as or better than his counterpart in private industry. The Commission has led the way toward the liberalizations of recent years although, in some instances, Congress has enacted liberalizing laws over the Commission's opposition. This is true primarily with respect to modifications in life insurance and retirement annuities.

Operating the retirement system for federal employees is one of the Commission's major programs. In 1920, Congress passed the Civil Service Retirement Act, which was amended numerous times since to bring it up to date. It now covers the majority of federal employees, including members of Congress. Under the Act, each employee with 30 years of service may retire on annuity at age 55; with 20 years of service, at age 60; and, with 5 years of service, at age 62. Everyone having 15 years of service at age 70 must retire. In addition, there are provisions for retirement due to disability regardless of age.

At the end of fiscal year 1968, there were 600,000 former federal employees and 250,000 survivors of deceased employees drawing annuities totaling approximately $2.3 billion annually. By the year 2000, it is expected that the number of annuitants will have doubled and they will be receiving $6 billion annually.

Because of the widespread interest among employees and also because members of Congress are covered by the program, many bills are introduced each year to modify the law, usually to extend the benefits. Analyzing each legislative proposal is the painstaking and time-consuming job of the Commission's experts in its Bureau of Retirement and Insurance. The retirement system is funded by employees and government each contributing a percentage of employee salary at rates fixed by law. The Commission tries to make sure that the system is actuarially sound—that the benefits to be paid are available. It scrutinizes each new bill and opposes those in which the benefits are more liberal than can be supported. Of great concern in recent years has been the fact that Congress has authorized more liberal benefits without a proportionable modification of the financing system. The Commission has forecast that the retirement account will become bankrupt by 1987 unless remedial action is taken. It has repeatedly called the matter to the attention of Congress but without success. If the present level of benefits continues, it is estimated that, without added financing, by the year 2000 Congress will be required to make an annual appropriation of $4 billion to meet the obligation.

Other employee-employer sharing programs administered by the Commission provide employees with life, hospitalization, and medical insurance. Unlike the retirement program, however, these are handled by contract with private companies. The Commission negotiates and monitors the contracts. In addition, it reviews the benefits in the light of changing need and what may be taking place in other employment jurisdictions, both public and private.

While the retirement and insurance programs are the largest employee-benefit activities of the Commission, other significant items receive continual attention. For instance, vacation and sick leave is always a hot issue. Each employee earns thirteen "sick" days a year, and there is no limit to the number of days that may be accumulated. Knowledgeable members of the staff as well as many federal managers are inclined to feel that the sick-leave privilege is widely abused. The Commission has made studies that tend to support this conclusion. But the Commission has shown no tendency to rush in with a quick answer, for almost any proposal for more restrictive change can be expected to draw opposition.

RECOGNITION OF OUTSTANDING SERVICE

In 1967, Shirley J. Gomora, an inventory management specialist at the Army Ammunition Procurement and Supply Agency, received a $5,000 cash award for making a suggestion that led to a saving of $10.4 million in expenditures for ammunition in one fiscal year. Although it was the largest cash award made to a single individual in 1967, it was only one of many awards and was by no means the largest ever given out. In 1956, Dr. William B. McLain of the Department of the Navy was awarded $25,000 for developing the celebrated sidewinder missile. In 1967, approximately $4,392,000 was paid to employees who made suggestions that resulted in savings to the federal service measuring $156,572,000.

The suggestions program, under which these awards were made, is one aspect of a broad activity administered by the Commission to reward federal employees for unusual contributions. Although each agency has its own program for recognizing its employees, the Commission provides the central leadership to assure that all programs meet acceptable standards. In addition, it promotes activities to assure that the award programs are integrated into the agencies' personnel management programs with the support necessary to make them succeed.

Over and above the suggestions program, each agency has several levels of award. By no means all involve cash payments. The top award in each agency is ordinarily for distinguished service by persons who have made outstanding work contributions to the agency over a period of years. The highest of all awards for distinguished service is the Presidential Award, made usually to five federal employees selected each year by an independent committee's review of agency recommendations. Normally, such awards are made only to individuals who have sustained careers of excellence while making outstanding contributions to the national welfare.

The Commission's Office of Incentive Systems is the liaison with agencies that have formal programs of recognition of outstanding public officials, which it promotes with great emphasis. Its twofold motive is a belief in employee recognition as good management—that awards are incentives for ideas that will contribute to efficiency of government or improvement of society—and a desire to draw attention to the day-in-day-out contribution of federal employees so that the taxpayer may have a better idea of the effect of his own contribution.

The career programs of the Commission are the efforts of many imaginative people both within and without the Commission to make the American taxpayer's own workforce efficient and responsive. They also reflect an institution in transition. They show the stern hand of the tight manager, the benefactor of the unfortunate, and the promoter of enlightened personnel management. They mirror the Commissions' entire, complex personality.

V

Enforcement:
An Exercise in Delicacy

Enforcement of the laws that it administers requires that the Commission review and judge the actions of other federal agencies and, when appropriate, assess penalties or apply sanctions that are directed toward job applicants, employees, federal agencies, or even state governments, depending on the circumstances. Handling alleged violations is tricky. Some are procedural; others involve sensitive character judgments. In many instances, the Commission must exercise its enforcement authority wisely enough so as not to tread on important toes in the path of justice. If the sound of its whip is sometimes more a thud than a crack, the politically astute in Washington understand. But, over the years, its actions have virtuously reflected a strong desire for excellence in staffing the federal service balanced with political realism.

CHEATING IN EXAMINATIONS

Cheating in examinations is not new. It is a problem of all testing jurisdictions. Through its many years of experience, the Commission has gone to great lengths to protect itself against violators. Perhaps its best defense is the size of the system itself. The numbers of possible test questions run into the millions, and there are various issues of the same examination, so it is difficult to know which set of questions will be used at any one of the 1,000 examination centers on a given date. The Commission does not claim that it is never out-witted, however, for some very ingenious persons challenge it. Nevertheless, each inference or allegation is doggedly investigated, and a few interesting cases have come to light.

One of the oldest examination frauds is impersonation—having a stand-in take the written test. A few years ago, an alert examiner compared the test papers of a person who had made a high passing mark with the same candidate's papers on a previous examination, which he had failed. The hand-writing was different. Investigators soon learned that the applicant's wife had received a passing grade in the earlier examination. A comparison of the handwriting on both husband's and wife's passing examinations showed that it was identical. The Commission representatives, confident of their success, then confronted the wife and charged her with taking the test for her husband. She denied the allegation with vigor and said that she had been attending a college football game in a neighboring state on the day of the examination and could not possibly have stood in for her husband. The Commission, checking the alibi, found it airtight, but it also found that her husband had gone with her to the football game. Now the Commission knew that he really had a stand-in for the examination but it did not know who. Finally, a sister of the wife was found to be a three-time winner. She had passed the test once for herself, once for her sister, and the third time, for her brother-in-law.

In proven cases of fraud, the individual is removed from whatever job he may have attained and is barred from future civil service examinations for three years. In addition, he may be referred to the Department of Justice for prosecution under statute.

FALSE CLAIMS

Cheating on tests is not all that the Commission must watch to protect the federal service against people who choose to circumvent rules and standards. The application for employment is a critical instrument that causes a wide range of enforcement activities. In this area, the Commission has two concerns. First, the examining processes depend on a candidate's truthful explanations of his background ability to perform the job he is being considered for. Second, the Commission must sensitively enforce the general standards of character and fitness required of all candidates for federal employment.

The following instructions from the standard job-application form are critical:

A false or dishonest answer to any question in this application may be grounds for rating you ineligible for federal employment or for dismissing you after appointment, and may be punishable by fine or imprisonment (U.S. Code, Title 18, Sec. 1001). All statements are subject to investigation, including a check of your fingerprints, police record, and former employers. All information will be considered in determining your present fitness for federal employment.

The candidate must certify that all the statements made in his application "are true, complete, and correct to the best of [his] knowledge and belief and are made in good faith." All statements are subject to investigation, which may or may not be exhaustive and, depending on the sensitivity and importance of the job, may take place some months after the person has been employed. Therefore, the Commission must rely heavily on what the candidate writes on his application form.

The grade in many examinations for high-level jobs is based on the candidate's experience. Sometimes the descriptions applicants provide of their past work require careful reading; sometimes some unusual things turn up. One applicant for an executive job, for instance, gave an impressive account of his business experience by explaining that he had been the owner-operator of a restaurant chain and previously had been engaged in an investment business. The chain of restaurants turned out to be two hot-dog stands, the investment business a small pawn shop. The examiners concluded that it would be difficult, if not impossible, to get anyone to agree that the man had violated the law, but they were certain that his actual experience was not sufficiently extensive to permit his eligibility in the examination.

In cases involving a skillfully written but exaggerated application, the Commission rates the candidate ineligible but ordinarily does not attempt to prosecute him as a law-violator. After all, it is in the American tradition for a man to put his best foot forward.

One of the most common, clear-cut falsifications is the claim of a fictitious college degree. Some years ago, one of the Commission's examiners was reviewing an application of a candidate for a top-level executive position when he noticed that the candidate claimed an A.B. degree with a major in business administration from the Chillicothe Business College, Chillicothe, Missouri, in 1929. It happened that the examiner had attended the same institution in the same year, and, at that time, it was nonaccredited and did not give an A.B. degree. The candidate was trapped by coincidence. Ironically, such a degree was not required in the examination, but the candidate's claim raised a question about his integrity and put his entire experience in doubt. An investigation revealed that he was an eminently well qualified man with a successful business background and was highly regarded in his community. The educational claim was a fiction he had been living since the Depression when jobs were almost impossible to get and many employers set unusually high educational standards.

Similar occurrences are commonplace. The Commission takes a liberal position and does not "throw the book" at a person if this indiscretion is the only thing found wrong with his application and if it is immaterial to the requirements of the particular examination. If the falsification was the thing that made him eligible for the job, however, the matter is treated much more seriously.

The high-water mark of embarrassment concerning falsified applications came to the Commission late in the 1950's when President Eisenhower appointed a new civil service commissioner whose qualifications were investigated by the Senate Post Office and Civil Service Committee. A point raised in the investigation was an allegation that the appointee had falsified his educational background in a previous application for federal employment. The charge that a commissioner who would share responsibility for the integrity of the examining system would himself take a federal job application so lightly of course made headlines in Washington. It was a particularly sensitive issue, since he had been appointed while Congress was in recess and was therefore actually serving in the job subject to Senate confirmation.

Compounding the Commission's embarrassment was the fact that its Washington examining division had previously rated the man in one of its examinations and presumably had a record of his application on file. The committee requested a copy of the application, but, to the distress of the Commission —particularly the division chief—it could not be found. The chief of the division, accustomed to clerks reporting that one of its thousands of applications was lost, had a standing rule that there was no such thing as a lost application. "It's not lost. Find it," was the standard response, which worked more than 99 per cent of the time. But this was the one time it failed. The most exhaustive search within the memory of any Commission employee did not produce the application. The division desperately wanted to find it; it had nothing to lose by producing it, and everything to lose if it appeared that it had deliberately mislaid it. The whole matter cooled, however, when the commissioner resigned, and the Senate committee dropped its proceedings.

PERSONAL CONDUCT

In addition to demonstrating that he can perform particular duties, a candidate for a competitive service job must show that he meets acceptable standards of character and fitness. The Commission uses the word "suitability" to cover charactor and fitness. When it determines the suitability of a candidate, it makes a serious judgment, for it refers not necessarily to the candidate's ability to perform certain duties with accuracy but rather to his worthiness to bear the title of federal employee.

The job-application form is used to obtain essential information that enables the Commission to judge sensitively. To make the task as easy as possible, the form contains a number of simple, direct questions requiring yes-or-no answers. For instance, the laws disqualifying anyone who belongs to an organization advocating violent overthrow of the government are the subject of one direct question. A false answer clearly calls for enforcement action.

Other questions and answers present more complex problems. The Civil Service Act specifically prohibited employment of anyone who habitually used intoxicating beverages to excess, and, until 1968, this was the subject of one question. But ascertaining what was "habitual" and what "excess" proved a little too much for the Commission. Although it has dropped the question from the application it is still concerned with enforcing this part of its law. It has concluded, however, that the job application is not an effective way to discover an alcoholic. Most persons who are so afflicted do not admit the fact on an application.

The Commission has found itself in many ticklish areas when applying and enforcing its own standards relating to personal character. During and immediately following World War II, there was great public concern over the conduct of federal employees. The Commission's standard that a federal employee could not engage in "open and notoriously disgraceful conduct" was interpreted very strictly, and many persons were removed or prevented from employment for conduct that was hardly open or notorious.

In one case, a man accused of being a homosexual chose to defend himself by discussing his attractiveness to the opposite sex and shoring up his position with numerous accounts of his amorous adventures. His arguments were so convincing that he was cleared of the charge of being a homosexual but nevertheless rated ineligible, since his admitted proclivities for the opposite sex seemed to exceed the acceptable norms in that direction.

Although homosexuals are still rated ineligible by the Commission, the general suitability standards are applied with much more sophistication today than they were two decades ago. There was a period when the Commission, in an effort to respond to what seemed to be public desire, may have opened private closets and made character judgments from evidence concerning the personal conduct of individuals, but, in recent years, it has shown a tendency to take no more note of an individual's private life than is absolutely necessary. The "open and notoriously disgraceful" standard has again become the rule.

In applying the "open and notorious" standard, the Commission tries to adjust to the mores of each particular community. What is acceptable conduct in one community may be different in another. Like it or not, an examination for postmaster, for example, is apt to bring out some of the colorful aspects of human conduct that require the Commission's evaluation.

A few years ago, two arch rivals were competitors for the job of postmaster in a small western community, a community so small that there were no strangers. One candidate was rumored to be carrying on extracurricular activities with a well-known woman in the town. The two candidates had places of business across the street from each other. One day, while looking out the window, Candidate A saw the woman in question approach Candidate B's parked, vacant car, get into the back seat, and duck down from sight. Shortly thereafter, Candidate B sauntered out, nonchalantly got behind the wheel, and drove out of town. Candidate A, seeing the opportunity to have a little fun at his competitor's expense, picked up a friend and together they went to the local airport where he kept a small plane. Shortly after takeoff, they saw the car parked in a normally secluded location and buzzed it a few times. Not content with having harassed Candidate B at such a time, he amused the town by telling the story. Candidate B became so angered that he accosted Candidate A in the presence of witnesses, pulled a gun, and threatened to shoot him if he did not button his lip. Cool heads dissuaded him, but, as he was angrily stuffing the gun back in his pocket, he discharged it and shot himself in the leg.

When the Commission was forced to review the circumstances, it demonstrated a certain amount of agility by not addressing itself to the moral conduct of Candidate B but to his emotional stability. It found him ineligible on the grounds that he was not temperamentally suited to the job of postmaster. It concluded that anyone who would so lose his temper and go for his gun might not be the most diplomatic representative of the government service, particularly if a patron of the post office chose to express a critical opinion of mail delivery, for example.

In another case, the Commission was forced to cancel the eligibility of a candidate for postmaster on grounds of character, for it had agreed that the candidate's conduct was both open and notorious. A woman had applied for the job of postmaster, passed the examination, including the ordinary investigative processes, and was about to receive the appointment, when the Commission received a letter that made them stop the proceedings and send an investigator to the community. The woman had included in her application as a significant part of her experience the claim that she operated a one-stop service station. In addition to the normal service-station and car-repair facilities, the business included a restaurant and sleeping accommodations. The letter alleged that the overnight "business" was considerably more extensive. Indeed, the Commission later confirmed that the manager herself occasionally helped handle the rush-hour traffic. In explaining the case to one of the civil service commissioners, a representative of the postal examining division said, "When we first reviewed the woman's application we wondered why, with that extensive and obviously successful business, she would want to be a postmaster. But when the full facts came out, we felt we understood. In operating that complete one-stop service station, she could sell everything but stamps, and she wanted that business too."

In this particular case, it could not be said the candidate had falsified her application, although some of the Commission's examiners felt that she had not complied fully with the instructions, which specify that applicants must list all experience they have had, beginning with the first employment. It was argued, though somewhat facetiously and irreverently, that she had omitted a significant employment history from her application. Even though the Commission has demonstrated compassion for people and their frailties, however, it seems safe to conclude that it would not knowingly permit the employment of the operator of a house of prostitution, even if the fact were honestly stated on the application.

AGENCY CONFORMITY

Much of the Commission's enforcement role concerns agency adherence to civil service regulations governing appointment, promotion, demotion, separation, and transfer of employees. In general, agencies have authority to take such actions as long as they conform to regulations, and Congress and the President expect the Commission to make certain that they do.

The Commission does this by inspecting agency personnel operations. The government is divided into "inspectable" units —approximately 2,000 across the country. Under a regular inspection cycle, each unit is visited by a team of inspectors once every four years. In addition, there are as many special inspections of individual units or groups of units as occasion requires.

In a routine inspection, the Commission takes a random sampling of individual personnel records and reviews the actions that have been taken. If it sees a promotion that appears procedurally questionable, it may make a study of the entire promotion operation of that agency. It also interviews representative numbers of employees, supervisors, and managers to ascertain their feelings concerning the policies and their application within the agency. This information may influence the course and extent of the inspection. Special inspections of an agency or group of agencies may result from complaints from employees.

Generally, agency personnel officers are so well trained and the top management is so knowledgeable concerning policy requirements that there is rarely a case of wholesale violation of the established requirements. If it does occur, it is normally in a small, independent agency, without the resources to employ a competent personnel technician, or in new agencies in which the top management is not yet attuned to requirements. Frequently, new agencies are charged with the responsibility of getting a program under way in great haste, which sometimes causes the requirements of personnel policy to be ignored, more often through lack of knowledge than through intent. Oftentimes, program objectives have been well thought out, but the administrative and organizational mechanisms have been taken for granted.

The Commission is always in a rough spot when a new

agency stumbles over regulations. The head of the agency usually has the sympathy of top management—it wants him to have every help possible in getting the new program launched. The Commission, likewise, wants to help, but it does not want to be accused of being a roadblock. The effect is that it operates with a certain amount of timidity, even though it may well be aware that trouble is brewing.

A case in point was the creation of the Office of Economic Opportunity. Commission representatives felt reasonably certain that OEO was headed for difficulty from the day it was launched—not because they thought partisan politics were controlling it, but because no management system was in control. They called the situation to the attention of agency officials but found little interest. Finally, news stories began breaking, and congressional criticism began to occur. When the Commission went on an inspection, it found a number of areas requiring serious attention.

When the Commission discovers serious violations, it faces delicate situations. If, for instance, it finds that the son of a U.S. senator has been promoted to a job for which he is not qualified—as it actually has—it faces one kind of problem. If it finds that the action in question was directed by a presidential appointee, it faces a different kind, though no less difficult. If it is one isolated case, it may get lost in a maze of negotiations; if it is a continuing practice, Armageddon may be faced.

In many instances, a call from the Chairman of the Commission to the responsible official is all that is required. If the responsible official chooses not to heed a call from the Commission, alternatives must be considered. It can apply sanctions. The Commission can, among other things, withdraw from the agency its authority for most of its personnel actions. This is rarely done any more, if ever, for a practical reason: the withdrawal authority would have to be taken on by the Commission itself, which does not have the staff. Since most of the inspected units are smaller elements of a large organization, the Commission now usually turns its facts over to the headquarters office, which takes the necessary corrective action.

Not long ago, in the course of a survey of the Equal Employment Opportunity Program, the Commission found that the merit promotion system was being violated in a field installation of one of the military departments. It turned its evidence over to the headquarters of the department and asked for a review and report. The department conducted an independent inspection and found that not only were the general policies of the program being violated, but so were those of the agency. It removed the head of the unit, and the Commission sustained the removal when the employee appealed.

In 1968, when the NAACP picketed the post office in Portland, Oregon, the Commission looked into the allegations of unfair and discriminatory promotion practices. It found that the post office had had to assign some employees temporarily to window-clerk work, pending receipt of authority to establish the jobs permanently. A year later, when authorized to fill the jobs on a permanent basis, they had to apply promotion procedures. By agreement with the postal unions, promotions go to the senior qualified bidder—the qualified employee with longest experience who wants the job. In this case, they established a requirement that one year as window clerk was necessary; therefore, only the clerks who had been temporarily assigned could meet the requirement. Overlooked were some otherwise qualified employees with long postal experience but not as window clerks. The Commission ordered that the jobs be readvertised to the employees, that the one year's window-clerk experience requirement be abolished, and that the promotion list be re-established. Any who could have been promoted under the new standard should be allowed to remain in the job; others would have to be demoted.

Generally, the Commission leans over backward to avoid

demoting an employee who has been promoted or assigned to a job through error, on the theory that he should not be penalized for what was not his error. It prefers to take whatever action is justified by the circumstances against the person responsible. Sometimes, however, an irregular promotion prevents a deserving person from moving up. In such instances, the only equitable action is to return the promoted employee to his original position.

Rarely does the Commission require removal or suspension of employees for violation of regulations, but letters of reprimand are rather frequent. In most instances, the Commission prefers to turn the facts over to the agency and request a report of its action. Usually the agencies take warranted disciplinary action without being directed to do so.

Toward a Common Goal

When inspections were first begun, they were largely confined to audits of personnel actions. As the Commission's role and interests have broadened, however, its inspections have also broadened, to encompass the wide spectrum of personnel management throughout the agency. Once they concentrated almost exclusively on the operations of personnel offices; now they encompass the actions, attitudes, and problems of top management, supervisors, employees, and personnel technicians.

Today, inspections stress how well agencies comply with the program emphasis desired by the Administration in office. If, as in the Kennedy and Johnson administrations, priority is on employment of women, then high on the agenda of inspectors is determination of whether women are being given fair consideration in promotion programs and the extent to which they are included in training activities.

Almost any personnel activity of an agency can become the interest of inspectors, on the well-established premise that the personnel program is a principal tool in the achievement of agencies' basic missions. When inspectors find a problem, they endeavor to isolate its cause. If it is rooted in general policy or Commission regulation, they seek change at home. If it is caused by the way in which the manager or his personnel officer is performing his job, they point the finger in that direction.

The Commission has tried to make its inspections as effective as possible. There is always a certain amount of apprehension about inspections and inspectors. The Commission must evaluate agencies, but it must also live and work with them. Consequently, both spoken and written diplomacy are important.

Every inspection culminates in a written report of findings and recommendations. Over the years, there has been continuing discussion within the Commission on the tone and content of the reports. Some feel the reports should be factual, extremely diplomatic, and uncritical of agencies except where criticism is unavoidable; others feel that they should be candid and pull no punches. For many years, the prevailing point of view was that, since the objective of the inspections was to gain compliance, more could be gained from informal negotiations than colorfully written documents. Public officials would listen and respond to straight talk, but criticizing their operations on the record where others could see would cause trouble and complicate future relations. As a consequence, the reports became so bland that persons not deeply involved in the inspections began to question their value. In addition, the managemement of some agencies in Washington, carefully reading the reports of their own field installations, took comfort if they were uncritical—sometimes more comfort than the circumstances perhaps warranted.

The whole report-writing process was thoroughly reviewed in the mid-1960's, when an official of the Department of Agriculture called the Commission's executive director and read parts of a Commission report on one of Agriculture's field offices. It was glowing. He followed this by reading an appeal from an employee of the same office, providing evidence that things were less than lovely. The executive director, himself a believer in hard-hitting reports, had proof, therefore, that responsible agency management would respect correctly critical reports much more than reports so bland they really told nothing. As a result, reports became much sharper.

Reports are the only tangible evidence that an inspection has taken place. Unless they reveal a fairly accurate picture of the scope, content, and findings of the inspection, the person whose knowledge must be confined to them can be either misled or left with an unsatisfied appetite. Their significance has increased as inspections have become more important to the top management of both the agencies and the Commission.

Inspections provide members of both the agencies and the Commission the opportunity for periodic personal encounters to discuss how they are getting on. Whereas the Commission, in its earlier days, may have evaluated various employing units of an agency at different times and submitted separate reports, it now strives to make a one-time total evaluation of an agency's personnel management. Inspectors conduct simultaneous reviews at various points throughout the field and in the Washington offices. Reports are prepared at each site inspected and are forwarded to the Washington office, where they are reviewed and compiled. The composite report is studied carefully to identify any pattern of actions, good or bad.

The final report is reviewed by the Chairman, an indication of its importance. The Chairman and appropriate members of his staff then meet with the head of the agency and his staff to discuss the findings. These meetings ordinarily do not take up individual errors or violations unless they are of unusual significance. The topics discussed are such broad matters as the quality of the agency's program for recruiting and developing personnel, strengths of its supervisory force, and the attitudes of employees.

PREVENTION OF POLITICAL ACTIVITY

The Commission is required to administer the law prohibiting partisan political activity by employees of the competitive service and employees of state and local governments whose jobs are financed wholly or partly by federal funds. Employees are not prevented from voting, making financial contributions to the party of their choice, or participating in nonpartisan local elections. They are, however, prevented from running for political office, participating in the management of political campaigns, using their position to influence the outcome of an election, and soliciting funds for political purposes.

The Commission is usually drawn into cases of political activity only when someone charges that an employee has violated the law. If the charges are substantial, it investigates the case and conducts hearings of both accusers and defenders. If the Commission finds that a violation has in fact occurred, it must order that the guilty employee be suspended or separated. Separation must be effected unless the three-member Commission votes unanimously for a lesser penalty. The minimum penalty is suspension for thirty days.

There is nothing more agonizing for the Commission than to be forced to take notice of an allegation of soliciting funds for political purposes in a department or agency. As campaign times approach, party financial machinery begins to shore up the coffers for the obligations ahead. The "$100-a-plate" dinner has become popular. With more frequency than the Commission cares to tabulate, it hears allegations of competitive service employees' being solicited by higher-ups to purchase dinner tickets. It is always a matter of concern, for, if an employee is solicited by someone higher than he is in the chain of command, there is always the possibility of coercion—the fear that, if he does not cooperate, his career will somehow be adversely affected. Solicitation violates the law, but the extent of the Commission's jurisdiction depends on whether competitive service employees are involved.

A celebrated case publicized in the Washington newspapers in the mid-1960's involved employees of the Rural Electrification Administration of the Department of Agriculture. Resolution of the case almost brought a serious confrontation between the Commission and the Department. After investigating the charges, the Commission became convinced of the facts of the case, but competitive as well as excepted service employees were involved. The Commission believed that the fact left no alternative to dismissal; the Department of Agriculture saw the case differently and refused to take action with respect to the excepted service employees over whom it had jurisdiction. The Commission was left with the hot decision of whether to force the Department's hand by requiring dismissal of the competitive service employee or to let the case ride. The Commission was saved by the timely departure of the employee for other reasons.

Any enforcement action involving politics is extremely delicate. Politicians do not like public embarrassment; it provides their opponents with too much ammunition. Members of the Commission obviously do not wish to take an action that will reflect adversely on their own party. Beyond that, it requires an unpleasant involvement with key members of the official family with which they must do business each day and upon whom they must rely for support in many areas. Nevertheless, the Commission faces the wind when necessary and takes action. Its annual report for fiscal year 1967 showed that it had required the removal of two employees and the suspension of six during the year. The violations ranged from distributing campaign literature to running as a candidate for a partisan political office. The report also showed that, since the passage of the Hatch Act in 1930, 3,938 complaints concerning the activities of federal competitive service employees had been investigated, resulting in 237 removals and 352 suspensions. The number of complaints that must be examined averages approximately 100 each year.

The law differs with respect to state and local government employees only in that the Commission has no authority to apply a penalty less severe than removal. If the Commission finds that the law has been violated, removal is required. However, the federal government cannot require a state to remove an employee; it must depend upon the state's voluntary compliance with its orders. Its only enforcement mechanism is the application of the sanction of withholding federal funds equal to twice the accused's annual salary. The state can then choose whether to pay the price in dollars or in scalps. The annual report of 1967 showed that two state employees had been ordered removed. During the same year, 72 complaints were received concerning the activities of state employees.

The Commission has moved swiftly but carefully in enforcing its standards. It must also defend and reassess its goals as new problems of public administration (such as those discussed in the next chapter) are identified.

VI

Into the Limelight

In addition to the three core programs discussed in the preceding chapters, the Commission has other activities, some little known and bearing little relation to the internal management of the federal service. One of the most important is defense of the federal service. Although this role is not usually described in printed statements of its programs, it is assumed to be essential to the Commission's responsibility as the central personnel agency. Early in the 1950's, the Commission, shocked by the force and extent of general criticism leveled at government employees, began to fear that the reputation of the service might be damaged so that able men and women would no longer wish to be associated with it. Under the leadership of Chairman Robert Ramspeck, a program known as the Truth Campaign was launched to set the record straight concerning federal employment and federal employees.

The Commission did not allow itself to be drawn into the controversy over individuals. It built its campaign on the strong belief that the majority of federal employees were competent and making significantly useful contributions. But more important was the principle that federal programs are so vital that the American people could not afford to have them in the hands of the corps of second-class workers that would result from constant unfair criticism and public ridicule.

Although no longer recognized as a separate campaign,

this type of defense is still carried out as integral to the Commission's work. Every Commission official assumes responsibility for telling the correct federal career service story whenever he sees the need or opportunity, but leadership flows from the Commission's Public Information Office. It presents facts and figures that show that the government employs high-caliber men and women who contribute substantially to the good health and welfare of the nation. It draws attention to employee contributions and, in an organized campaign, makes federal employees better known in the communities where they work and live.

Because the Commission has assumed the role of defender of the service, it must also accept the role of apologist. It cries out in justifiable anger when a false or unsubstantiated charge is leveled at the service, but it becomes alarmed when a bit of administrative untidiness is discovered in the family. Usually allegations of mismanagement or corruption, always attendant on public administration in a free society, involve the performance of employees. Consequently, even though a problem may lie entirely within another agency, the Commission rarely escapes some involvement, however minor, when the problem is given a public airing. So frequently does this happen that, whenever a news story breaks in which an agency or an employee gets unfavorable publicity, the seasoned Commission staff member immediately begins to anticipate questions and delves into the records so as to be ready for the inevitable telephone calls. If not from the press or a member of Congress, he is almost certain to hear from the person next above him in the Commission's chain of command, who likewise has been reading the newspapers and wants to be prepared with answers.

APPEALS

From its earliest days, the Commission has carried the major responsibility for assuring the correctness and fairness of its own staff's decisions. In addition, it has always been responsible for examining the circumstances of an employee's removal when it is alleged to have been made for such improperly discriminatory reasons as political affiliation, race, or religion.

Most appellate matters used to concern actions during examinations. The cause of the appeal was usually a low or a failing score or a disqualification for unfitness. In recent years, however, the law and executive orders have greatly expanded the appeal rights of employees, so that now almost any agency action adverse to an employee is subject to review by the Commission. "Adverse" action has been interpreted as removal, reduction in rank or pay, and suspension for longer than thirty days.

Most appeals are received, evaluated, and decided by appeals examiners or officials of the appropriate bureau or regional office. When an appeal concerns a charge of racial discrimination, however, it is taken directly to the Board of Appeals and Review in the Washington office. The Board has final appellate jurisdiction for most cases, but some decisions, such as those regarding an examination rating in the field service, cannot be appealed above the regional office. Although the decisions of the Board are final, appellants sometimes request the commissioners to reopen a case. The commissioners then review the record, and, if they decide that there is sufficient cause for reopening, they request such additional investigation as they consider necessary to making a decision. They rarely reopen a case, attesting to the over-all thoroughness of the process.

BIRMINGHAM, ALABAMA: EQUAL EMPLOYMENT?

Sometimes the Commission finds itself in the position of agent-promoter within the federal family, for, whenever a President calls upon employers for help in solving a problem, the federal government, as an employer, must respond quickly or even perform as the model. Response to such calls is normally given a separate identity, and even organizational and staffing adjustments are made, to assure that it receives proper attention. The programs and the emphasis change as the interests of an administration or the needs of the country change. Although such special activities are not new, the dramatic demands for social change and the role of employment have unquestionably seen a more intensified development of special-emphasis activities in recent years. In effect, these programs have extended the Commission's role and responsibilities into new areas or areas previously considered within the domain of the Chief Executive.

In the spring of 1963, events in Birmingham, Alabama, brought change to the Commission. Private employers were asked to employ Negroes in jobs previously closed to them. Representatives of the Justice Department, trying to achieve racial harmony in the troubled city, were met with the challenge that private enterprise was doing as well as the federal government. The reaction was immediate, and a call to the Civil Service Commission brought an embarrassing response: it did not have immediately available statistics on the racial composition of federal employment in local communities. Before the day was over, a man from the Commission's Washington office had gone to Birmingham to look into the federal government's posture there, and all agencies with Birmingham offices had been instructed to notify their people to cooperate with him. Until then, the Commission's role in equal-employment opportunity had been one of support rather than leadership. Responsibility for leadership and administration of the program rested in the White House under a presidential committee.

The Birmingham experience taught the Commission that it had been perhaps too complacent and had taken too many things for granted. It had felt reasonably secure that the open competitive examining system was antidiscriminatory, representing one standard applied equally to all. The way to obtain a job in the federal service was to compete in the appropriate examination when it was announced and make a score high enough to be within reach of consideration when a vacancy was open.

But, in Birmingham, it was found that subtle deficiencies could creep into the process. If there were few vacancies but an adequate supply of manpower, there was little need to give an examination wide publicity. Press releases announcing a new examination had been discontinued, because newspapers had paid little attention to them. Little turnover in federal jobs had made aggressive recruiting efforts unnecessary. The way to learn of an examination announcement was to watch for it on bulletin boards in a post office or some other federal office building.

The Commission found that Negroes in Birmingham had little confidence that they would actually have an opportunity to be employed even if they had been aware of examinations. Also, there was evidence that they might even be unaware of the long-standing practice of announcing examinations on bulletin boards. The Commission concluded that the some-what limited publicity given to recruitment left it vulnerable to the charge that the system was not really open and that, even though the system might be fair when correctly operated, a large segment of the population lacking confidence in it meant that there was a change to be made.

Subsequently, a series of surveys was initiated in cities with concentrations of federal agencies. Teams of Commission employees examined every aspect of federal employment in the various communities. Statistics were gathered about local employment problems and practices. The surveys were conducted in the full light of publicity. The press was informed, and a complete cross-section of community and civil-rights leaders was interviewed. The local educators were consulted and, in some areas, even deficiencies in the educational system were identified. Although the reports were intended as working documents for internal government use, they were in fact candid expositions of the community and contained, for some of the communities, probably the most comprehensive compilation of data any Washington agency had. They became best-sellers in the agencies responsible for solving urban and civil-rights problems. They pinpointed the ghetto problems of some big cities. Some even identified areas that were to become headlined trouble spots in later years. A retrospective look at the Los Angeles report, for instance, showed the potential of Watts in Los Angeles.

Chairman John W. Macy, Jr., was not shy about bringing problems identified to the attention of the agency responsible for action. He referred problems in education to the Department of Health, Education, and Welfare, employment-service problems to the Department of Labor, and weaknesses in agency programs and even attitudes of local managers to the heads of the agencies concerned. The Commission did not hesitate to point the finger at its own operations. It reopened many examinations and revised its recruiting publicity system. It also strengthened its inspection and review of agency operations.

In September, 1965, President Johnson transferred from the President's committee to the Commission the responsibility for the Equal Employment Opportunity program for federal employment. In his executive order, he charged the Commission with the task of developing a model program, another expensive activity for the Commission. Not only did it have the difficult, sometimes delicate, task of consulting with civil-rights leaders and federal agency representatives, but it had to put teeth in its program by issuing regulations and enlarging its agency-inspection agenda to ensure compliance.

New Voters in the South

Probably few people associate the Civil Service Commission with the registration of voters in the South in the 1960's. This is understandable, because voter-registration and public-personnel administration appear to be unrelated subjects. That the Commission was required to play an extremely difficult and sensitive role in this unusual federal activity must go down as one of its most anomalous assignments.

When the Voter Rights Act of 1965 was passed, much publicity was given to the fact that, under it, the federal government would send examiners into political subdivisions of some states to assure that registration would accord with the law, but the Act's requirement that the Civil Service Commission would have to conduct the activity went largely unnoticed. Although the Attorney General was responsible for determining where and when examiners would be required, the Civil Service Commission would by law actually compile the voter lists. In addition, the law made the Commission responsible for conducting hearings on challenges to registrants when necessary. It required the Commission, when requested by the Attorney General, to appoint observers to the polling places on election day to watch both the casting and the counting of ballots.

These were functions that the Commission did not seek or want and in fact it saw no profit in them. There was little to gain from success and much to lose from failure. However, both the planners in the executive branch and the leaders in Congress recognized that an existing agency with a record of aloofness from partisan politics, experience in rendering objective judgment, and detachment from the controversy leading to the legislation would have to carry out the Act. In addition, the agency would have to have an extensive field organization and supervisory capacity. The Civil Service Commission was the agency that most nearly fit these specifications.

When the law was enacted, there was little time to recruit and train new personnel who could be entrusted with such delicate operations. The Commission therefore decided to use its corps of investigators, a carefully selected group already trained to meet unusual situations with diplomacy.

Because of the intensity of feeling in some southern states, apprehension concerning the operation extended even to the personal safety of the men and women involved. Although it was impossible to provide certain physical protections, extraordinary machinery was established to keep the Commission informed and in contact with its personnel assigned to the task. All interested Washington agencies were anxious. The Commission established a command post that looked like a small war room, manned it constantly, and received reports from all points at all times. Not only was it possible to know what was going on in each location, but the Chairman was able to keep the Attorney General and the President informed on the exact status of the activity at any time.

Under the law, this supervision is a continuing Commission function, and, by January, 1968, voter-listing operations had been carried out in 108 locations in 62 counties in Alabama, Georgia, Louisiana, and Mississippi, with slightly more than 158,000 voters listed. Observers had been at the polling places in 17 elections. Because the Commission had to use its trained core of personnel, the program was carried out not without some cost to its basic programs, but it acquitted itself with distinction and won the plaudits of the Attorney General. It is particularly significant that the Commission did its job with such a high degree of anonymity.

EQUAL RIGHTS FOR WOMEN

Many people remember the delightful exchange at one of President Kennedy's press conferences when he was asked by a well-known female member of the press what he was doing to keep "the promise of the Democratic platform to work for equal rights for women, including equal pay, and to wipe out job-opportunity discrimination." The President responded, "I'm sure we haven't done enough. I must say I am a strong believer in equal pay for equal work and I think we ought to do better than we are doing, and I'm glad you reminded me."

The question was far from new. On January 7, 1895, Commissioner Theodore Roosevelt had written in a letter to Miss Carrie Harrison of Wellesley College:

> No distinction is made in the examinations, or in any proceedings under the Commission, between men and women. They compete on precisely the same basis. The sole discretion whether men or women shall be appointed rests with the appointing officer, the Commission certifying persons of the sex called for. Most appointing officers seem to prefer men, about in the proportion of four to one.

Through the years, the question as to whether the federal service really has given women equal treatment in employment has periodically caused political leaders to look to the Commission. The Commission has, in turn, had to report.

In the Kennedy Administration, the matter began to receive great attention in all phases of our society. The President appointed a commission under the chairmanship of Eleanor Roosevelt to study the status of women. Employment was only one major aspect of the study. Since the federal government is the country's largest employer and since it is one area about which the President could be expected to do something directly, it was logical that it would receive special emphasis. Chairman Macy was named to the Commission on the Status of Women as a member of its committee on employment.

His committee made an exhaustive study of federal employment and found that, although many women were federally employed, some of the statistics were nevertheless embarrassing. The percentage of women in the higher grades and in managerial positions was low. The problem was identified as formidable. The seeds of discrimination were deeply planted, and it would take more than conversation to bring about a change.

It was necessary first to find and remove whatever made discrimination easy. In this case, nothing was wrong with the law; the Civil Service Act spoke against discrimination on the basis of sex. However, under a long-standing opinion of the Attorney General's office, agency appointing officers could specify male or female in its eligibility requirements when requesting a civil service register. It was assumed, of course, that an appointing officer would properly decide whether a job required men or women only; it took only a cursory review of the requests for certification of males, however, to show that there was little or no justification for many of them. The question was resubmitted to the Attorney General, who interpreted the law in a different way from his predecessor of many years earlier. His opinion formed the basis for new procedures: agencies were required to show why they thought it necessary to limit a position to a particular sex.

Special review procedures were instituted at the Commission, requiring that each request for certification by sex be evaluated by specialists. A tough line was taken, and some interesting practices came to light. Some were justifiable, but others represented only the whims of appointing officers. That the new requirement was imposed surprised some old-line bureaucrats, and it took a while for them to believe that the Commission really meant business. Nonetheless, the number of requests to fill positions with "men only" fell to less than 2 per cent.

This review procedure was only a step, though. It covered only one mechanical phase of the initial employment process. There were many other things that required attention, from job-qualification standards to training and promotion practices to the attitudes of the federal managers who make the ultimate employment decisions.

When President Johnson took office, he let everyone know that he expected action, and the Commission made certain that the massive federal employment machinery was attentive. First, the Commission called for reports, touching off a great race for statistics. Every federal executive began looking at his rolls to see how many women were on them at what levels in his organization. Most people are sensitive to the desires of top management and they began looking for something to report. Consequently, a certain amount of competition developed, and there were undoubtedly more appointments and promotions of women to key positions than would otherwise have occurred in a like period.

President Johnson set an example by appointing several women to key posts at the political executive level. However, the number of women appointed to top levels in the career service continued to be embarrassingly small. Federal executives said they had difficulty finding qualified women program managers because few women had come up through the ranks and few had received training in the program to be managed.

But, as the problem has been long in development, so the solution will require time. The Commission wages a continuing campaign to redress the balance, and top management of the agencies also sees the desirability of achieving the President's objectives. Progress is being made, but as the newswoman reminded President Kennedy, so future administrations will probably need to be reminded.

"OPERATION DOLLY"

The decisions of Presidents Kennedy and Johnson to use the Commission for assignments formerly handled by the White House added immeasurably to the Commission's stature, but also added hours of unbudgeted workload. The assignments ranged from thankless chores to programs of great importance, but agencies, like people, cannot have a thing both ways: if they want the influence that goes with proximity to the position of power, they must be ready to perform when a call comes.

Shortly after President Johnson took office, the director of the Commission's Bureau of Recruiting and Examining was attending a meeting in the office of the executive director when a note was placed in front of him saying that Chairman Macy wished to see him at once. This was unusual; the Chairman normally does not interrupt such meetings. In their brief discussion, the Chairman reported to the Bureau director that he had just received a telephone call from "a very highly placed person" concerning the immediate need for a top-level secretary at the White House. Names were not mentioned in the conversation, but it took no unusual powers to realize that the "highly placed person" had in all probability been the President. Thus an operation unheard of in Commission history began. The director of the Bureau of Recruiting and Examining, to whom the responsibility was assigned, realized that, through this simple process of finding a secretary, the Commission as an institution and its capabilities could come under the scrutiny of a very important judge. Consequently, the operation was conducted with the greatest secrecy and at the highest levels. Given the code name "Operation Dolly," it caused both consternation and amusement.

The bureau director contacted agency personnel directors and requested them to supply the names and personal histories of employees who not only could meet the highest secretarial qualifications but also could be released by the agencies on immediate notice. The secretaries would have to possess the highest technical competence and the finest personal attributes, and they would have to be free to work the long and sometimes unpredictable White House hours. Personnel directors were told to discuss the inquiry with no one but those who "had to know." That the White House was looking for a secretary would not only have made news copy, it would have brought a deluge of applicants—mostly from the unqualified. It was also emphasized to the personnel directors that their failure to provide the best could result in embarrassment far greater than could possibly occur from merely displeasing the Civil Service Commission; the Commission—at least the director of the Bureau of Recruiting and Examining—was not about to take sole responsibility. The persons referred by the agencies were interviewed and, in some instances, tested, regardless of their already established reputations. The Commission wanted to take no chances.

As might be supposed, the list that was developed was short, even though the government is large. The director and deputy director of the Bureau kept it with them at all times, night and day, awaiting a call from the White House to arrange for further interviews there. The ladies on the list were also asked to stand by. Despite all the effort at careful planning, one oversight caused a near catastrophe at zero hour. The expected call came unexpectedly on a Saturday morning, and it requested that the candidates be at the White House within half an hour. The candidates had not been asked to stay at home by the telephone over the weekend. Only one of them could be reached and she only by the closest of chances—she was walking in the door of her apartment with an armload of groceries just as the telephone rang. The Commission staff members felt that they had been literally saved by the bell, though, for the young lady got to the interview on time and was accepted.

The incident had twofold significance to the members of the Commission's staff who were involved. First, it demonstrated the President's interest in competence. Second, it was the tip-off that the President expected the Chairman of the Civil Service Commission to be his chief personnel adviser on all matters small and large. It was among the first of many unprecedented assignments from the White House involving the Commission's staff.

A Broader Management Role:
Federal Executive Boards

The presidential job of managing the executive branch, with its multiplicity of programs affecting every segment of society, presents incomprehensible problems. Consequently, as the Commission has moved closer to the White House, it has found itself involved in the solution of general managerial problems to an extent beyond what was formerly considered its normal operations.

The federal executive boards are an excellent example of the expanded management role of the Commission. Students of federal government administration have long believed that more coordination among federal agencies at the local level would serve the public better and provide significant economies. The agencies have different field structures to meet their specific requirements, and each agency is responsible for its own relations with the public. Some have regional jurisdictions, a region comprised of a group of states; some have state offices that report directly to Washington. Still others have district jurisdictions over portions of states. Even those having regional jurisdictions do not have the same regional boundaries. This multiplicity has tended to result in a group of autonomous federal services at the local level. The problem of informing the field service on Administration programs is cumbersome and sometimes slow.

The Kennedy Administration, believing that there was need for rapid communication of philosophies to key people in the field, where program administration actually takes place, decided to establish interagency working groups outside Washington. On November 10, 1961, a Presidential memorandum to the heads of departments and agencies directed the Chairman of the Civil Service Commission to establish a board of federal executives in each of its ten administration regions. The following significant paragraphs are from the memorandum:

> As an integral part of present steps to increase the effectiveness and economy of Federal agencies, I want coordination of government activities outside of Washington significantly strengthened. . . .
>
> Although each Executive agency and its field organization

has a special mission, there are many matters on which the work of the departments converge. Among them are management and budgetary procedures, personnel policies, recruitment efforts, office space uses, procurement activities, public information duties, and similar matters. There are opportunities to pool experience and resources, and to accomplish savings. In substantive programs, there are also opportunities for a more closely coordinated approach in many activities, as on economic problems, natural resources development, protection of equal rights, and urban development efforts. . . .

As a first step in bringing federal officials outside of Washington closer together, I have directed the Chairman of the Civil Service Commission to arrange for the establishment of a Board of Federal Executives in each of the Commission's administrative regions. . . .

The cooperative activities of Federal Executive Boards must be undertaken primarily through the initiative of the heads of our field activities. The Chairman of the Civil Service Commission and the director of the Bureau of the Budget will furnish the Boards from time to time with guides on official goals and objectives in the management field and will arrange for periodic briefings by national executives of the government. . . .

Following a reasonable period of evaluation of these initial steps, recommendations are to be prepared by the Chairman of the Civil Service Commission and the director of the Bureau of the Budget for continuing improvement of the management and coordination of Federal activities.

In the light of subsequent activities, the emphasis on program coordination was probably the most significant point in the memorandum. In addition, the responsibility placed on the Chairman of the Commission and the director of the Bureau of the Budget to make recommendations for continuing improvement of the management and coordination of federal activities was important.

The establishment of federal executive boards was not an entirely new idea. In 1921, the Bureau of the Budget had established federal business associations at various federal employment centers across the country. They had been orphaned, however, and cut off from official lines of contact with Washington for many years. Many had continued to exist largely through the interest and voluntary efforts of field personnel. Membership was not limited to the heads of field establishments, and the activities of some were merely social, consisting of periodic dinner meetings. As such, these centers did not constitute a dynamic organization.

After the federal executive boards had been established, it was decided to encourage, though not require, the reconstitution of the federal business associations as organizations consisting primarily of heads of field establishments or executive personnel. There are now approximately eighty such organizations, called federal executive associations, and fifteen federal executive boards. Although the boards are more closely tied to the managerial line from Washington, the associations are also given a great deal of attention. They receive most of the communications sent to the boards and are requested to undertake projects similar to those of the boards.

Establishing and continuing the interagency effort through the boards and associations has become an integral part of the Commission's program. Board chairmen report progress on projects to the Chairman of the Commission, and, as their activities have developed, it is obvious that much more is involved than improved use of office space or telephone services.

Although initiated by President Kennedy, the boards were embraced by President Johnson, who took the unusual measure of addressing the board chairmen directly by letter. He personally called upon the members of the federal executive boards to involve themselves in implementing programs to achieve the goals of the Great Society. He stated: "The demands of the future are no less challenging than those of the past. I expect each member . . . to make the Federal Executive Board an even more effective instrument for progress in meeting our goals."

The boards have been asked to undertake a number of

projects, but among the most significant is the work on critical urban problems in their areas. In January, 1968, the President's Council on Youth Opportunity, under the chairmanship of Vice-President Humphrey, called a conference in Washington of the mayors and prominent citizens of the fifty cities with the most critical problems. The involvement expected of the chairmen of federal executive boards and associations was underscored by the fact that they were brought to Washington to participate in the conference, and while they were there, the Chairman of the Commission gave them priorities for action in the ensuing year. Items listed were employment of the disadvantaged, city redevelopment, crime prevention, and law enforcement.

It is not strange, of course, that field officials were asked to help, in view of the problems facing the country in 1968, but that federal executives from the field service were charged with responsibility for such action by the Chairman of the Civil Service Commission reflects the uniquely specialized extent to which both the Chairman and the Commission as an institution were serving the President.

On November 1, 1965, President Johnson directed to the heads of departments and agencies a memorandum expressing his desire that all aspects of public service be improved. The memorandum said, among other things:

> The task of government is to serve the public. It has been my deep and continuing concern to assure that each American receives from his government the fastest, most efficient, and most courteous service. As our society grows more complex and our population expands, we must explore every path in our quest to provide the best possible service for our individual citizens. . . .
>
> Some months ago I asked Chairman Macy of the Civil Service Commission to survey our existing practices and to suggest ways to improve our efforts. He has reported that progress has been made. But we must continue to forge ahead, for in a real sense we have only begun. . . .
>
> The time for action is now. This is particularly so in view of

the new programs recently passed by Congress which reach all of our people.

I am today placing Chairman Macy in charge of a new and concerted government drive aimed at bringing better service to our individual citizens. I am directing him to coordinate the activities of each department and agency and to report to me every 90 days on our progress to improve the quality of service and to make the government more accessible to the people it serves.

It was a unique assignment for the Chairman of the Commission, one that at first glance would seem to have little relationship to the normal function of the Commission, but some staff members were eager to come to grips with it. Feeling responsible for defending the image of the federal career service, if for no reason other than to facilitate recruitment activity, they believed that there were many areas that could be improved by changing attitudes and procedures without material increase in cost.

There is nothing to get action from the bureaucracy quite like the requirement of a periodic report to the President. In this case, the President had asked for reports from the agencies every ninety days. Effects of their suggestions have been far reaching and range from such elemental things as diplomatic letter-writing and telephone courtesy to extending office hours. Every agency has re-examined every aspect of its contacts with the public. The Smithsonian Institution started keeping the museums open to visitors until 10 P.M. during the spring and summer tourist seasons. The Department of Agriculture consolidated offices at the county level to provide one place for the agricultural community to go for service. The Government Printing Office opened retail bookstores both in and outside Washington, making federal publications available for sale for the first time outside the facility of the Superintendent of Documents.

Perhaps the most dramatic of all moves, however, was the inauguration of one-stop federal information centers in major metropolitan areas, so that inquiring citizens would know where to go to find answers. Centers have been opened in such widely scattered locations as Atlanta, Chicago, and Kansas City, Missouri. The project offered the federal executive boards an excellent opportunity to improve government service coordination in the field in line with the objectives originally stated by President Kennedy.

VII

A Cooperative Effort, a Multiagency Job

The tasks of the central personnel agency are so enormous that many groups, agencies, and individuals must be involved if they are to be accomplished. The Commission's actions and the policies over which it presides have such significant effect on the way agencies conduct their business that it would be impossible for the relationships to exist free from controversy. Yet, controversies that do develop are normally conducted in a low key and rarely get beyond the walls of the agencies involved. The Commission knows that its day-to-day working relationships with agencies can easily affect its success—or failure—on another matter, perhaps a more important one, on a succeeding day.

The Commission is seen by Congress as a quasi-independent body, by the President as a strong right arm of the executive branch. These dual roles make it the object of both envy and pity. It is in a position of great power; yet, for its success, it must have high cooperation from those over which it must be powerful.

In its dealings with the agencies, the Commission has to wear many hats. With respect to its regulations, it is enforcer, viewing transgressions with distaste, while with respect to many agency actions, it is judge and jury. For the executive branch, it is an advocate, frequently persuading agencies to adopt positive action programs that may seem inconsistent or unrelated to the Commission's basic function. It advises. It counsels. Occasionally, it cracks the whip on the errant. It is a guardian of merit, but it must live and succeed in a practical political world where standards of merit are neither absolute nor universally practiced. For these reasons, it must be flexible. Because of a desire to overcome an old image of negativism, it has shown remarkable ability to recognize and get aboard a new bandwagon, sometimes to the dismay of those who would rather not even have a parade, let alone be drawn into it. It can·exhort and harangue and twist arms to get agencies to increase employment of minority groups within the rules, and it can just as easily sputter with horror when an agency gets into the headlines for going too far in the process.

To the sophisticated personnel director or federal manager who understands the political facts of life, such actions are understandable and a matter of course. But to the uninitiated, who view public administration from the pages of a textbook, they are as inconsistent as are those of the parent who swears at his son for using profanity.

As it is a wearer of many hats, the Commission must occasionally take one of them in hand, go through an agency's front door, and ask for help or peddle its wares. It neither seeks nor gets an appropriation large enough to support all the programs for which it is responsible, and, for many of its accomplishments, it must rely on the cooperation of the other agencies. This is particularly evident in civil service examining, where several thousand specialists are officially accredited by the Commission as examiners to rate papers in their fields of expertise. Their prompt availability is vital to the process. The Commission is dependent upon them. And they greatly outnumber its own staff. The Commission could not hope to have on its own staff enough professional personnel who are abreast of all technological developments in the many occupations found in the federal workforce.

Examining is the only Commission function for which its staff is directly augmented by agency personnel, but there are other Commission programs in which agency financial support is vital. Training, for instance, is almost entirely dependent upon reimbursement, as is the largest part of the investigative program.

In recruiting and examining, the Commission operates a service that supplies the many federal programs with the new personnel they require. Agencies specify the number of people desired and the kind of skills required. It is the Commission's job to see that the orders conform to general requirements and that they are filled on a timely basis. It knows that it must make its service satisfactory to its customers.

The Commission's job affects nearly every agency in the federal family. Depicting the various relationships is difficult because there are so many people involved and so many subjects on so many levels at so many locations. Without question, however, the Commission's job must be a cooperative effort.

The operational network is vast. The Chairman and the other commissioners are in constant contact with the heads of agencies, and staff at the political level who report to them, as well as with the many subordinate officials and employees. The executive director has a wide range of contacts, particularly at the levels of assistant secretary and director of personnel. The bureau director's contacts are normally with assistant secretaries, directors of personnel, and specialists but are by no means limited to them. Regional directors have daily contact with the heads of field establishments and subordinate personnel officers. The contacts multiply in Washington and the field at lower levels, where the day-to-day transactions take place. Over-all, there are approximately 2,000 points in the agencies, exclusive of the Post Office Department, in which employment authority is exercised.

THE PERSONNEL FRATERNITY

Today, there are more than 37,000 persons working on the specialized business of personnel administration throughout the federal service, at an annual cost of more than $353 million. These numbers do not tell the full story, however, for they do not include many clerks, typists, and stenographers in personnel offices, nor do they include the administrative officers who, though not classified as personnel specialists, spend large amounts of time at personnel work. But they do indicate that here indeed is a specialized group of people large and important enough to have its presence felt in almost every corner of government within the executive branch.

In 1938, agencies were required by executive order to establish a division of personnel supervision and management headed by a director of personnel. The order spelled out the functions of the division and the duties of the director. The natural follow-up to this was the establishment of subordinate personnel offices throughout the agencies wherever significant hiring activity takes place. Now, almost every office in which hiring authority is exercised has a personnel office. Such offices range in size from one consisting of a single technician and clerk to large offices with professionally trained specialists in such fields as labor relations and employee counseling.

At the top of the personnel profession in the agencies are the directors of personnel in Washington. They are the focal point of the Commission's contact with the agencies on personnel policy matters. Their jobs are unique, and, as a group, their relationship with the Commission has been both historic and colorful.

Late in the 1930's, the executive order that required agencies to establish the job of personnel director also required that those appointed be members of the influential

Federal Council of Personnel Administration, the interagency group whose chairman reported directly to the President. As suggested earlier, the new personnel directors provided much of the leadership that resulted in change in personnel policies and practices. Imaginative and aggressive, the new directors organized a professional society that did much to encourage the training and development of young people who desired to specialize in personnel work.

But as might have been expected, their presence was not universally acclaimed. Old-line, practical-minded administrators sometimes viewed them as long-haired theoreticians. Some careerists in general management occupational fields undoubtedly reacted with a certain amount of jealousy, for the newcomers had a unique, almost untouchable status. They had the force and prestige of an executive order that backed their individual positions within their respective agencies and also gave them the added responsibility collectively to advise on policy as members of the Council.

The Commission's staff, likewise, was not immune to strong feelings concerning the new directors who represented the force of change—much of which was directed toward the Commission. Nevertheless, there had to be close contact, with or without mutual admiration. The Commission's staff represented old and new philosophies. The new tended to identify with and support the directors of personnel; the old were more inclined to consider the new directors as interlopers. Institutionally, the Commission reflected ambivalence.

In 1954, the relationship was dramatically altered when Congress abolished the Council and the executive director of the Commission was given the task of consulting with agencies on policy. The personnel directors were then organized into an interagency group to advise the Commission, not the President.

The present-day director of personnel has an extremely difficult job. He must recognize the importance and power of the Commission. Normally, the head of an agency would not think of appointing a new director of personnel without contacting the Commission. Usually, the agency wants someone in the job who has, or can command, the respect of the Commission, and the director of personnel is expected to be the official link between the agency and the Commission. He or his subordinates must interpret the Commission and its policies, procedures, and decisions to the agency, a most unpopular assignment if the Commission's actions restrain the management of the agency in some action it may wish to take.

The director's job is greatly influenced by the interests and attitudes of the agency head. If the latter has a good understanding of modern public administration and is interested in personnel administration and the merit system, the job of the director of personnel is greatly simplified, both within the agency and in dealing with the Commission. If, on the other hand, his boss is relatively disinterested in personnel matters, impatient with procedure, and unconcerned with the merit system, the personnel director is destined for a period of "life in the middle." If he identifies too closely with the Commission, he risks being looked upon as something of a fifth columnist; if he get too aggressive in support of an agency position that the Commission feels is clearly wrong, he is likely to be considered less than effective by the Commission. The position is sensitive and requires great balance.

Although the Commission does not view the large corps of agency personnel directors, officers, and technicians as members of its own staff, it recognizes that its own success as the central personnel agency is in no small measure affected by the manner in which they perform. Therefore, it feels a special responsibility for seeing that they get the necessary instruction and support to handle their assignments adequately. But it does not assume responsibility for the performance of the individual agency employees; its instructions are directed toward the agency with the expectation that the agency management will assure itself of competence among its personnel technicians.

The Commission's routine means of communicating the rules, regulations, and instructions that comprise the working federal personnel policy is the publication of a forbidding document known as the *Federal Personnel Manual*. Published in looseleaf form for easy supplement and expansion, it fills several binders. The personnel technician in the agency is supposed to know "the book" and properly apply it to the day-to-day problems he encounters.

Although the Commission maintains the public stance that it is in no way responsible for the actions of agency personnel technicians who carry out the policies and procedures, it does so with considerable difficulty. It is cited as the authority for so many decisions that to many an agency operating official his personnel office is "the Commission." Many times it is held accountable for actions that it may be totally unaware of. In Washington, for instance, an official of an agency not infrequently calls the Commission to complain about a delayed appointment, promotion, or transfer, only to learn that the necessary papers are still with his own personnel office and may not even require Commission review.

Another difficulty the Commission has had is overcoming its old reputation of being more interested in applying regulations than in getting new programs under way. Although it has sponsored many new ventures and written new flexibilities into the rulebook, it occasionally unhappily discovers that the personnel technicians in some agencies are not applying the new regulations. The Commission understands that anyone who has to draw attention to a restraining rule or regulation is at times going to be unpopular, and for this reason it tries to give the agency personnel technicians full backing. When it learns, as it did in the mid-1960's, however, that some of its new flexibilities were not known to, or being applied by, technicians, it shows concern.

At that time, the Commission began receiving so many complaints about the interference of the personnel processes with the management of programs that it concluded that it should play a more positive role in influencing the quality of the corps of agency personnel technicians. It quietly set up an internal study project and classified it somewhat facetiously as the "improving the breed" project. It lost its facetiousness, however, when the executive director decided that the time had come to export it to the public, which he did by sending up a trial balloon at a luncheon meeting of the Washington chapter of the Society for Personnel Administration.

Among other things under consideration was the requirement that the appointment of every personnel officer at the middle and upper levels of federal service receive the prior approval of the Commission. Under the existing procedures, agencies had been free to promote or transfer whomever they chose to positions below the top executive levels as long as the individuals met the qualifications standards. The reaction to the executive director's statement was swift and antagonistic. The fraternity, as might be expected, was not happy with the implication that their quality needed improving. While backing away from some of the ideas contained in the executive director's trial balloon, the Commission held to the position that some course of action was necessary. As a result, a long-range program was hammered out in cooperation with the agencies. (It is discussed in Appendix A, "Career Opportunities in Personnel Management.")

The Commission's responsibility to sponsor improved personnel management has ruffled some agency personnel technicians. Since preaching is the traditional method of spreading the gospel, some of the Commission's staff have followed in the highest traditions of the circuit rider: they have preached. Those who raise their eyebrows at this question not the need for improved personnel management but the qualifications of the Commission's staff as theologians. They cite the fact that few members of the Commission's staff have ever had experience as operating personnel officers high in an agency. They further tend to feel that the Commission does not always practice its own preachments by introducing more new blood into its own staff at the executive levels when it has vacancies. Some feeling still exists that the Commission suffers from inbreeding.

These are problems that time will undoubtedly alleviate but not eradicate, for the nature of the business and organization is such that there will always be strains and stresses as opinions differ. However, the relationship today between Commission and agency personnel technicians is healthy and candid.

THE INTER-AGENCY ADVISORY GROUP

Important to the Commission's relations with the other federal agencies is how it consults with them on matters of mutual concern. It has the responsibility of consulting before making a change in personnel policy or introducing a major new program. Beyond that, consultation is desirable, although sometimes difficult, to assure that the new policy is feasible and acceptable once promulgated.

The official vehicle for consultation is the Inter-Agency Advisory Group (IAG). As was pointed out earlier, it is composed of the directors of personnel of the major departments and independent agencies in Washington and it reports to the executive director of the Commission who chairs its semi-monthly meetings. Its meetings are rigidly held to ninety minutes in length unless there is an unusual problem to consider.

It is a large and diverse body. Agencies represented range in size from the Farm Credit Administration, with less than 200 employees, to the huge and sprawling Post Office Department, with more than 700,000 in its workforce. The personnel director of the small agency is usually a one-man band with little or no professional staff. Consequently, he is interested in the nuts and bolts of personnel procedures. The personnel director of the large agency may preside over a personnel program that employs a professional personnel staff as large as or larger than the Commission's. He is interested in only the broadest policy questions and may be totally unfamiliar with procedural detail.

Because of this diversity, *ad hoc* committees are generally established to consider new proposals or particular problems. Sometimes, the Commission presents to a committee a completely worked out proposal for its review; other times, it may present a raw question or problem for the committee to consider and propose a solution to.

Committee members are appointed by the Commission. They may consist of the IAG members or specialists on the agencies' staffs designated by the directors of personnel. Sometimes, committees may consider a problem for several months and may meet many times in the process of acquainting themselves with all aspects of the problem. The final proposal, which the Commission may put before the full IAG for official reaction, may or may not be in accord with the views of a majority of the committee members. The Commission believes that the purpose of consultation is not merely to gain permission to put a new policy into effect but also to make certain that the agencies' advise on the particular program's impact or workability has been fully considered.

Since not every member of the interagency group can be on every committee, some members may first learn of a proposal when it is presented at the meeting. Frequently, the Commission briefs the group on a proposal and schedules discussion at a subsequent meeting to allow the members time to study it and get the reaction of their subject matter specialists or other agency officials who will be affected by it.

In general, directors of personnel are sympathetic with the Commission's problems of consultation; however, they maintain a state of wariness. If the Commission neglects to follow the thorough consultative process or for some reason attempts to hurry it, they are quick to blow the whistle. The Commission has learned that it can be a fatal mistake to surprise them with a cake already baked. Only rarely does a policy question develop with such urgency that time is inadequate for employing the full consultative processes in as deliberative a manner as is generally desirable.

Even though directors of personnel are not bashful about letting the Commission know their feelings if they think they have not been consulted fully on a matter, they also know that, in any interagency meeting, they have the opportunity to speak out against any proposal and that the Commission has on many occasions modified its position after encountering opposition in the IAG.

Over the years, members of the smaller agencies sometimes felt badly overshadowed by the larger agencies in the IAG. Many times, their point of view seems to get lost in the shuffle. The cost of a policy that is being considered may mean nothing to the Department of the Army but possible bankruptcy for a small office with little money to spend.

Recently, the Commission has inaugurated a new effort to solve the problem by dividing the agencies into four groups and placing agencies of like size and similar problems together. The executive director and key members of his staff hold a quarterly luncheon meeting with each group in a private dining room maintained by the Commission. There is no planned agenda; meetings are informal. Topics range from details to matters of greatest importance.

In another effort to assist the small agencies, the Commission has grouped them into a committee under the leadership of its Office of College Relations and Recruitment, to assure that their programs are properly emphasized in the Commission's over-all college recruiting effort.

OTHER CHANNELS OF CONSULTATION

Some matters are so important and sensitive—large expenditures of funds, for example—that it is necessary for the

Commission to consult with agency officials in addition to the directors of personnel. In the largest departments, this is the assistant secretary for administration. In smaller agencies, it may be someone working under the title of executive director or director of administration. Such officials are responsible for the personnel management as well as the fiscal management programs of the agencies. The Chairman may sometimes consult with agency heads or undersecretaries; in the most unusual or important circumstances, he may have a subject placed on the agenda of a Cabinet meeting.

Sometimes the Commission has dealings with department officials, such as the heads of bureaus or laboratories, who are highly placed and widely known but subordinate to the policy levels of the department. Such contacts, although essential to the Commission, are filled with administrative hazards.

Some years ago, for example, the Commission found it was supplying cover for a mini-rebellion. Four of its boards of civil service examiners, having a common thread of interest in that they were all recruiting research personnel, but for different departments, formed an organization that they called the Associated Boards of Examiners. The organization met annually to exchange views. One board was in California; the others were in Washington.

At first, the Commission showed no special concern for the activity and even lent some encouragement to the idea. It became a little puzzled, however, when it realized that it was being considered almost an outside party by the organization within its own family. Its concern increased when it found that the annual meetings were being used as semipublic forums for employees to air their grievances against their own management or even Presidential policies. The Commission was not concerned about a public airing of grievances against it, for it was used to this. But it saw little profit in sponsoring a forum criticizing the policies of the President and Cabinet officers as well as Congress. It ordered the organization disbanded but set up an advisory committee of boards-of-examiners representatives, so that they might have a means of presenting their views to the Commission through an official channel. However, the Commission scrupulously kept the appropriate agency personnel directors fully informed by inviting them to participate in each meeting.

This period marked the beginning of a unique relationship between the Commission and the federal establishment that has involved practically all levels and offices of the Commission. Particularly interesting has been the Commission's involvement with scientists in the federal service. After Russia launched the first satellite late in the 1950's, there was great and continuing concern with the government's research programs, particularly in the physical sciences. Scientists wanted freedom from many of the managerial restraints placed on them by the rigid federal personnel system, which some of them felt was not always appropriate to productive research effort. They were also concerned that competition from private industry would drain the federal service of its best research talent. The Commission found itself being held publicly accountable for many of these things, although at the time it had no control over them.

Of necessity, the Commission found itself paying greater attention to the heads of research laboratories and their subordinates, even though they were but small parts of larger agencies. Many of the problems disturbing scientists were related to personnel. Consequently, the Commission has expanded rather than diminished its activities in the field. In 1962, for instance, it made a special review of the personnel programs and policies being applied in a number of laboratories. It found a wide misunderstanding of personnel procedures. Some things the scientists felt were impossible could be easily accomplished; others were prevented by agency policies.

The basic problem was communications. The research laboratory in a California military installation was a long way from headquarters and sometimes subordinated under several layers of command containing no scientific personnel, so its administrators felt that there was no one who would give a sympathetic ear to their problems. The situation was eased by an arrangement worked out with the chief scientist on the staff of the Secretary of Defense. Through its regional directors, the Commission identifies problems for the chief scientist who, in turn, evaluates and refers them to the departments of the Army, Navy, and Air Force. This is an unusual role, but the Commission seemed forced into it by the peculiar nature of the problem and the feeling that, as the central personnel agency, it had to fill a vacuum. By the most careful footwork, the Commission keep personnel directors fully informed of its actions and findings, but maintaining balance requires constant attention.

The Field Organizations

Over the years, a tendency developed in some agencies to leave personnel matters to personnel people. If the agency head had a personnel officer, he considered it that man's job to deal with the Commission. There was also a tendency in some agencies to consider everything the Commission dealt with as routine personnel matters. Today, many of the problems the Commission has found itself having to consider touch on such sensitive issues that it has been forced to insist upon the personal participation of the heads of the field establishments.

When the Equal Employment Opportunity Program was intensified after the Birmingham crisis and the program of community reviews was launched, the Commission insisted that agency heads be involved, at least in the interagency meeting beginning each survey. Some head-knocking was required—particularly in the military agencies. In a number of instances, the first meetings were attended by either a low-ranking staff officer or a low-grade civilian personnel officer, despite the Commission's request that the head of the installation or his deputy be present. The Commission did not overawe the military commanders, who were in the habit of paying attention only to orders through their own chains of command. However, when the Commission went to the top levels of the military departments in Washington, the commanders in the field who had not recognized the importance of the Commission's earlier request found themselves receiving instructions to cooperate.

When the Commission launched its program to establish the interagency boards of examiners, it had realized that success would depend in large measure on the support and involvement of top agency management throughout the field. (See Chapter III.) It insisted that not personnel officers but heads of field establishments staff the boards, since the boards were largely executive bodies designed to support activities and provide only broad guidance to ensure responsiveness to agency needs. Additionally, the Commission believed that the field head of an agency had no more important managerial function than recruiting qualified personnel and that his involvement through helping to oversee the examining activity would provide him with the opportunity to make his desires effective.

There was some adverse reaction. Some personnel officers felt they were being bypassed; some agency installation heads felt they were too busy and too much involved with their own program administration to devote the time to such activities. But the Commission was adamant; the line was held with few exceptions.

The recent trend toward group activity in solving problems has been based upon the belief that some federal programs could succeed only through the combined energies and leadership of the agency heads in the field. Each head of a field installation reports to a regional or Washington office, sometimes many echelons down from the Cabinet or Presidential-appointee level. Directives from the top go through many heads and sometimes many interpretations before they reach him. Programs that require a coordinated or community effort require central leadership, but in many communities there is no central leadership, although there may be significant federal agencies.

The boards of examiners were not the first interagency action promoted by the Commission, however. In the mid-1950's, for example, many federal agencies were recruiting on college campuses. There was no coordination. Because it was both confusing and inefficient to have separate examinations for jobs requiring similar abilities, training, and experience, the Commission organized interagency programs presenting the total federal story with no single agency losing its identity. The Commission was becoming more and more a coordinating body responsible for marshaling the total resources of the federal agencies for attack on a common personnel or managerial problem.

When it was realized that greater attention had to be devoted to summer employment of young people, the Commission assumed leadership to assure that the federal service was showing the way in communities where it was a significant employer. It set up interagency committees under the federal executive boards, established earlier by President Kennedy. (See Chapter VI.)

A variety of approaches were employed. The President's Council on Youth Opportunity, chaired by the Vice-President, was responsible for the effort among all employers, so, in this instance, the Commission reported to the Vice-President. The Commission issued procedures to the agencies for achieving the objective but went beyond that to ensure that goals set by the Council were met. It dealt directly through its regional directors to see that the word was spread throughout the field. Committees were relied on heavily in major metropolitan areas to advise on the practicality of the procedures but, more importantly, to ensure that the approach was coordinated and that community agencies dealing with the youth employment problem would have one point of contact with the federal government.

If success can be shown by numbers, it may be revealed by the fact that, according to Commission reports, more than 116,000 people between the ages of 16 and 21 were given temporary employment during the summer of 1968. Of this figure, more than 78,000 were hired under a special authority for the disadvantaged, in work paying $1.60 per hour—which brought a separate set of problems to the Commission. (See also Chapter VIII.)

STRANGE PARTNERS

No discussion of the relationships between the Commission and the other federal agencies would be complete without mentioning the extraordinary tie-in with the Post Office Department. To many American citizens, the Civil Service Commission has been a man behind a window in a post office, since one of the anomalies of the federal government is that civil service examining—the stanch opponent of politics in employment—has largely been overseen by what historically has been one of the most political of all federal agencies. Until the Commission consolidated its boards of examiners into sixty-five interagency boards and put the personnel under its appropriation in fiscal year 1967–68, the Post Office Department was spending more for civil service examining for the Commission—not for its own jobs—than the Commission was.

Even now, although there are many other centers where information about federal employment opportunity and application forms may be obtained and notices of open examination are posted, the post office is still the place to go in most communities outside the major metropolitian areas. The personnel who discharge the duties are regular post office employees, trained and accredited by the Commission as examiners. They give out information about examinations and actually administer written tests when required to do so. They also arrange for the space in which tests are given at a thousand points outside Washington.

This arrangement has been in effect for many years. Until recently, the Commission has shied away from giving it thorough study or establishing serious contact with the department concerning over-all manpower requirements and the operation in general. The Commission has expected service from the Post Office Department, and the department has delivered it. The quality of the service has varied somewhat as the qualities of facilities and personnel have varied. However, some of the modernized Commission's staff members believe that the traditional post office no longer presents the image desired for the total federal civil service; although the post office once was an emblem of prestige and opportunity when the government workforce was largely clerical, it is so no longer. Also, the post office is no longer the central community gathering-place that it was in former years. Citing the urbanization of the nation, some Commission staff argue that supermarkets, for example, would be more logical places to reach the greatest number of people.

Admitting the logic of some of the arguments, the Commission has nevertheless had to measure them against other pragmatic considerations. Until recently, it has felt that, even though the system has recognizable deficiencies, the problems of gaining a divorce would be more troublesome than continuing the marriage. One of the interesting little mysteries of Washington is why the Bureau of the Budget, the General Accounting Office, or one of the appropriations committees of Congress has not insisted upon a full ventilation of the matter.

The problem has not been kept entirely hidden. Some years ago, the Post Office Department estimated the cost of its civil service activity in response to a congressional question concerning its nonpostal functions and, shortly thereafter, asked the Commission to consider relieving it of the burden. It was the first time that the question had surfaced between the two agencies at the national level. The Commission requested the Department to delay consideration, since it was then reviewing the entire examining function. Although it has begun to improve both examining and job-information facilities through its sixty-five interagency boards, it realizes that even these efforts still need to be supplemented in outlying areas for the public convenience. Thus, the postal service may still provide the best country-wide answer even today; its facilities and personnel are probably more uniformly located in relation to the population than those of any other agency, and, to replace them, the Commission would have to provide both space and manpower. In many areas, moreover, the job is not a full-time one but is done in conjunction with postal duties.

The Commission deals with the Post Office Department in a way different from its dealings with other agencies, chiefly because that department has its own body of law and regulations covering personnel matters. Some of the laws are rooted deep in the history of the postal service. It has a separate pay system. Postmasters' appointments are covered by separate law. An executive order issued by Woodrow Wilson still in effect requires that postal inspection be balanced fairly between Republicans and Democrats. This requirement alone imposes a political consideration in appointment. It would be little wonder if politics did not occasionally affect other areas of personnel selection. The Commission establishes the standards under which the majority of postal employees are hired and enforces application of merit procedures in selection. If it finds in its inspections that improper practices have entered the promotion procedures, it requires appropriate corrective action.

DYNAMICS OF MODERN GOVERNMENT

Like its programs, the Commission's interagency relationships are influenced by the dynamics of modern government. The relationships will undoubtedly change as the Commission's role changes or as government emphasis changes. This can be particularly true with respect to the groups with which the Commission has to deal. Late in the 1950's, when the public's major concern was with science, the Commission found it necessary to spend a great amount of time with scientists and their problems. A decade later, the problems of the cities and the ghettos shared the spotlight with rocketry, space, and electronics. Another decade will no doubt bring a new set of problems for democracy to face, and with them will come new relationships.

VIII

Life in the Cross Fire

"If you can't stand the heat, stay out of the kitchen," one of the many pungent quotes attributed to former President Truman, would be appropriate advice for anyone coveting an executive job with the Civil Service Commission.

With a federal civilian workforce of more than 2.5 million, reaching into the remotest sections of the country and around the globe to carry out every conceivable kind of activity, and with another 3 million job applicants considered each year, the Commission operates day in and day out in an atmosphere heated by urgent requests for action. Many times an action desired by one person dissatisfies another. As a result, the Commission is caught in a continuous crossfire of pressures, demands, and issues. Problems range from those caused by the sympathetic intercession of influential persons for individuals in need of help to those resulting from massive group action in behalf of a major policy.

It is difficult to portray accurately this aspect of the Commission's daily life because of its complexity and variety. Hence, this chapter consists largely of a series of incidents, episodes, and cases from whose descriptions it is hoped the reader can obtain a reliable view of some of the problems the Commission encounters and how it reacts to them.

SPECIAL INTEREST GROUPS

The Commission knows that articulate groups—some large and powerful, some small but influential—both in and out of government are important, and it encourages dialogue with them. There are, of course, all kinds of groups—unions, veterans' organizations, as well as numerous professional societies—with which it stays in close touch. Organizations in personnel and public administration are particularly noted. Commission staff members are encouraged to participate in such organizations to further their own professional development as well as to support the organizations and their objectives. Many of the societies have publications and sponsor forums in which public administrators exchange views with each other and with participants from college and university campuses.

Some of the most important groups outside government with which the Commission deals represent educational interests. The Commission's ties with them are based on several very practical considerations. From the colleges and universities come thousands of recruits each year for the labor pool, and the Commission considers it vital that the public service gets its share of the best. Naturally, the Commission would like the educational curricula to reflect the needs of government agencies. As the personnel requirements of the federal service change to meet the demands of society, it is important that those who train for the service have an opportunity to be fully aware of projected requirements. Hence, the Commission wants college faculties to have the widest possible understanding of the problems and challenges of government work. Many of the ideas and much of the support for improvement of the public service have come from academic circles. Although no one group can represent all higher education, the most numerous contacts the Commission has are with deans and professors of public administration, political science, and business administration.

The Commission promotes and sponsors many meetings, seminars, and symposiums in which both academic and government representatives participate. In the New York area, a college and federal agency council has served for many years as a forum for ideas, and somewhat similar approaches have been made in other sections of the country. In addition, Washington is in almost continuous consultation with the academic community, particularly with respect to the Commission's training programs. The Commission has to be careful that it does not weight its actions in favor of one group, for, within such a large complex as a modern university, there are groups with conflicting points of view and interests; it is practically impossible to satisfy them all. As a result of the numerous opportunities to speak and write, a steady flow of ideas, criticisms, and commendations flow into the Commission from the academic world.

Many organizations with the capacity for quick, forceful response watch the Commission, and sometimes it is forced to take actions that it knows will bring strong reactions. When it does, it announces its decisions and awaits the storm. Thus, in the mid-1950's, when the Commission exercised its newly received special authority to adjust the in-hiring pay rates for engineers and physical scientists, because trained professionals were in short supply, it started a fire among biological scientists that has yet to be fully extinguished. The pay of the majority of such jobs is determined by the Classification Act. Each job is graded according to the scope and level of its duties, and within each grade there are pay "steps." Each person entering a grade must enter at the minimum step. In 1954, Congress amended the law to give the Commission authority to permit hiring at steps above the minimum for positions in which recruiting shortages existed and it was believed that additional pay would help solve the problem.

The authority was immediately exercised for those job categories in which the government was having extreme recruiting difficulty, and where it could be shown that salaries were lagging far behind those of other employers.

From comprehensive studies and abundant statistics, it was clear that engineers and physical scientists were scarce but biological scientists were not. Civil service registers of physical scientists and engineers were depleted; registers of biological scientists contained a bounteous supply. The Commission could take only one action: it raised pay rates for engineers and physical scientists but not for biologists.

Almost immediately, letters and telephone calls came from all parts of the country. Officers and professional societies wrote on behalf of their members, and an individual letter-writing campaign ensued for a number of months. The biological scientists interpreted the action as a downgrading of their branch of science. Misunderstood, overlooked, or just ignored was the fact that the law did not permit the Commission to raise the rates of pay of biological scientists simply because there was an ample supply of them available at the existing rates.

The pressure groups are of many kinds. Two decades ago, the Commission began to give recognition to the problem of employing homosexuals in the federal service. Its position has always been clear and unequivocal: known homosexuals are rated ineligible and their hiring is not permitted. The Commission believed that its position on the matter was in accord with public opinion, and its concern was to see that procedures for keeping homosexuals out of government service were fool-proof.

But time has brought changes. A subject that a few years ago was discussed in hushed voices is now openly treated by the press and other news media. Recently, the Commission has had the unexpected task of defending its hard-line policy, which people have begun to question and attack. So open have protests been that a group representing an organization of homosexuals picketed the Commission's Washington headquarters, claiming that federal employment policies were unfair and, in 1968, there was a small but organized correspondence campaign to change the policy. The homosexuals have been joined in their protests by others who consider the policy an unfortunate example of improper discrimination.

The Commission has continued to hold its ground, but the protest, too, continues.

THE CONTRACTING-OUT CONTROVERSY

Expressions of concern about the size of the federal workforce accompanied the government expansion that began in the 1930's and continued through World War II. Congress attempted to contain the expansion during the Korean conflict by setting a ceiling on the total number of permanent employees. When the Eisenhower Administration took office, the feeling was widespread that government was competing with private enterprise by performing work that should have been done under contract. Consequently, a movement began to get large amounts of work out of the agencies and into the hands of private contractors.

Because federal salaries were lagging and industry was not hampered by the restrictions on federal employment, this approach was attractive. Private companies could hire anyone they chose and pay whatever they considered necessary. Although there were some restrictions on maximum salaries, there was much greater flexibility than in the federal service. New companies formed whose primary business was to serve the government. The research agencies of the military departments were among the earliest and largest to use private contractors. Later, the National Aeronautics and Space Administration (NASA) made extensive use of contracting services.

There is little doubt that contracting-out created competitive bidding for personnel, with the federal government sometimes actually bidding against itself. Direct evidence of the extent of this problem appeared when the Commission was requested to approve promotions for several employees of the Department of the Army, members of a rocket-firing team at Cape Canaveral, who were about to leave to take jobs in private industry. The Commission learned that the prospective employer was an Air Force contractor working at the same location. The Air Force was engaged in rocket research, just as the Army was, although it followed different work methods.

The Commission was unhappy about the situation, but there was little it could do at the time. The desire to keep the number of employees from growing, combined with other matters, largely interest in employment flexibility, outweighed concerns about the rather technical question of arrangements under which work is performed. Nevertheless, practices became so extreme that the Commission had to stop them. Situations developed in which employees, working side by side on the same type of jobs, were on different payrolls, one public and one private, with different conditions of employment. Some agencies even contracted with private employers to supply secretarial personnel. Unions and the congressional committees expressed concern, but what was "right" or "wrong" turned on interpretation of the law. The Commission ordered contracting for the employment of stenographers and typists stopped, and its general counsel issued a controversial ruling on the kind of work that could be contracted out. In general, it required that jobs needing close individual supervision by federal employees be performed by federal employees.

The battle lines began to form when the General Accounting Office, the watchdog of efficiency in government, began to examine personnel contracts in the course of their inspections. In 1963, they reported on the use of contract personnel at the Fuchu Air Force Base in Japan and asked the Commission to give its views on the legality of the arrangement. After thorough study, the Commission's general counsel held that the use of contract personnel under the circumstances was contrary to law, citing a somewhat similar case in 1962, when the Commission had required the Agency for International Development to cancel a contract with Kelly Girls for furnishing a stenographic and typing service.

In 1967, the General Accounting Office examined the contracts in effect at NASA's Goddard Space Flight Center near Washington. Again the Commission held that the contracts were illegal, in that an employer-employee relationship existed between the government and the employee of the contractor. Individual contractor employees were supervised by civil service employees.

Relations between NASA and the Commission became delicate when a NASA installation at Huntsville, Alabama, reduced its workforce from among the civil service personnel. The union charged that the people working on the federal payroll were being discharged, while others doing the same work on the contractor's rolls were untouched. The union secured a court injunction staying the decision until the Commission and NASA got together and worked out acceptable procedures.

The general problem is still largely unsolved. The feeling exists that there are many contracts throughout the Defense Department that do not conform to the legal opinion of the Commission. The number of employees who would be added to the federal payroll if these contracts were canceled would be several hundred thousand. From the taxpayers' point of view, great dollar savings would probably result. Private-enterprise overhead charges and profits are substantial. Business interests, however, believe they can do the work more cheaply and are not about to give up without a fight. The contractors are organized and prepared to exercise whatever influence they can at the highest policy-making levels. In opposition to the contractors are the powerful unions. There is also the ever present political problem of the size of the federal workforce. The 90th Congress restricted all agencies to the number of employees each had on the payroll on July 1, 1966. If a federal manager has a job to do and the dollars with which to do it, heavy pressures will be exerted to extend the use of contract procedures if he cannot employ more federal personnel. It is likely that the Commission will continue to be pushed and pulled from all sides on this issue for some years to come.

THE CASE OF THE CARELESS LIEUTENANT

The promotion examination for the Metropolitan Police Department of Washington, D.C., has long been a bothersome problem for the Commission. All policemen who wish to advance in rank must take the examination, which is given every two years and consists largely of questions on police regulations and procedures. Separate lists are established for each officer grade. The examination is highly competitive, and the scores are sometimes very close. A fraction of a point may make the difference between promotion and waiting two years for another review.

Because it is so competitive, the results are frequently challenged. Until recently, after the scores were released, each competitor was allowed to look at his paper under supervision, so that he could be assured that his score had been computed fairly. The chief of the Washington Examining Division once classified this part of the operation as "the peep show."

A few years ago, a lieutenant taking the examination overlooked several questions in the morning session. He finished what he thought was the complete set of questions with plenty of time to spare and spent the remaining time reviewing his answers. He noticed his error just as the examiner called time for the luncheon recess. The morning's booklet had to be turned in, and a second was to be issued for the afternoon. He asked to stay to answer the overlooked questions. The examiner refused, because only a specified amount of time was allowed for each part of the test. The lieutenant was naturally distressed and talked about the incident. Almost immediately, the Commission was requested to resolve the problem in "fairness to the lieutenant." The pressures came first on the Washington Examining Divison, whose chief reviewed the case but decided that there was nothing he could do. Later, several congressmen and senators, including members of both the House and Senate Post Office and Civil Service committees, were heard from, all sympathetic toward the lieutenant.

All three commissioners reviewed the circumstances but the original answer had to stand. There was no way the lieutenant could be helped without an injury to someone else. No other competitor had made the same error, and it had to be concluded that the instructions had been clear. If the lieutenant were given more time, every other competitor would have to be given more time, but, since the other officers had interpreted the instructions correctly, it would be unfair to require them to reassemble.

SUMMER JOB TROUBLES

Early in the 1960's, the Commission found itself in a difficult situation that had grown out of the steadily increasing interest in summer employment for students. How to handle short-time temporary employment in the competitive service had long been a problem. The Commission had considered the desirability of improving procedures for summer employment but felt that the only solution was to fill the jobs through a competitive examination. Since the Commission was having difficulty achieving what it considered to be a satisfactory program for permanent career hiring, however, it could not see the wisdom of diverting a large amount of its limited financial resources to such a short-time venture as summer hiring. It elected to turn the matter over to the agencies by authorizing them to make noncompetitive appointments totaling not more than 700 hours of work in any calendar year.

As both tuition costs and enrollments soared, parents became more and more interested in their sons' and daughters' having summer jobs. The situation was particularly acute in Washington, where most jobs require office skills such as stenography and typing. A few agencies, however, had small intern or trainee programs that offered opportunity to a fortunate few for a challenging summer experience. There were just enough of the intern jobs to create the impression that Washington was filled with such opportunity.

Two pressures began to build. One was from students and parents throughout the country for first-hand opportunity to learn about government by participating in it during the summer vacation. This group was concerned more with experience than with income. The other pressure was from students and parents in the Washington area, who were primarily interested in earning money. Since the government is the dominant employer in and around Washington, it was logical that students there would look to it as a major source of summer employment. They were, of course, not concerned with the principle that federal jobs in Washington should be distributed fairly among the citizens of all states.

Although there were some rumblings of dissatisfaction, the problem of reconciling these viewpoints was given low priority by the Commission—until someone in the Kennedy Administration saw interesting possibilities in it. Without consulting the Commission, the White House set up an office to operate a summer employment program. Agencies were asked to list jobs they wished to fill; names were considered for listed vacancies. The program appeared to have political overtones, but the White House office responsible merely stated that it was filling a vacuum, since there was no central point where a young person could learn about opportunities or be referred to agencies. It received relatively little critical attention until near the end of the summer, when all the students working in Washington gathered on the White House lawn, where President Kennedy spoke to them. The newspapers reported several thousand in attendance.

The following year, the program was continued notwithstanding increasing numbers of questions by members of Congress and articles in the press. Two charges were made, both of which were disturbing. One was that the White House was using summer jobs for political purposes and rewarding individual members of Congress, and the other was that most summer jobs were going to the sons and daughters of federal bureaucrats.

The Commission was caught in the middle. First, it had no facts. By deliberately keeping out of the summer employment program and leaving it to the agencies, it knew neither the numbers of persons hired nor the recruiting procedures of the agencies. It was not so naïve as to be unaware of which agencies did some hiring, but, beyond, producing an annual pamphlet explaining that it was necessary to contact the agencies directly, it devoted no resources to summer employment.

The charge that favoritism was playing a role in the selections was one the Commission could not ignore, however, even though it was said that an office of the White House was involved. That fact only made the problem more delicate. The Commission had to act.

Since 1883, the answer in such situations had been to give a competitive examination, but the Commission was not in a position to conduct examinations on short notice. It takes planning and dollars to operate a nationwide examination, and the Commission still did not believe that it was practical to conduct a large-scale operation for short-term employment. Its only recourse was to attempt to control by regulation. Accordingly, it restated the ban on political influence and, to give it meaning, required the agencies to utilize merit procedures for making summer appointments, spelling out general guidelines to frustrate political rigging. Summer plans had to be approved by the Commission in advance.

When these regulations were issued, the Commission was applauded in the press for its courageous action, which was interpreted as applying the brakes to a White House office. But there were knowing smiles from the politically astute, who appreciated the discomfort of the Commission at being caught in such an unhappy predicament. On Capitol Hill, some members of Congress were still not satisfied. Congressman Lindley Beckworth of Texas had introduced a bill that would have required a competitive examination for summer employment in Washington and apportionment of jobs among the residents of the states according to population. Although the bill did not go very far the first year, there was a warning in it.

The Commission's first regulations applied only to Washington, since that was where the problem seemed most intense; however, special investigations of agency operations were conducted nationwide during the summer of 1963. The Commission found some surprises. The allegations that sons and daughters of government civilian officials and military officers were receiving favored treatment were true. At a few military installations, the jobs were even doled out on the basis of the rank of the fathers. A colonel's son or daughter would be given a job ahead of the offspring of a captain.

The findings so distressed the Commission that the following spring it issued amended regulations requiring a continuation of merit plans in agencies but adding an anti-nepotism requirement. It prohibited any agency from employing the sons and daughters of employees and members of the agency's uniformed forces. This time there were cheers and tears—cheers from political leaders and the public at large, cries of anguish from the bureaucrats who had been taking advantage of the situation.

The Commission had a difficult time holding the line, for the regulation was not accepted without resistance. At the IAG meeting in which it was first announced, one personnel director said, "Does this mean that a 100-year practice in a particular installation where son has followed father into the work by breaking in during the summer will have to be discontinued?" The executive director answered, "If that's the practice, then a 100-year tradition just went down the drain."

The greatest pressure campaign came from a surprising source—the foresters. Many of them were in isolated locations where job opportunities were limited. They mounted an extensive letter-writing effort and employed the normal tactics of putting on the heat, but the Commission held firm.

Pressure for change also came from the unions, particularly the postal unions. They were concerned not over application of the policy to the higher-ranking employees but over application to those of lowest rank. Union representatives felt that there should be some relaxation so that the sons and daughters of the lowest-paid postal employees could work in a post office during school vacation periods. (The same point was made about the sons and daughters of enlisted personnel of the armed forces.) The Commission was sympathetic, but it did not yield. It felt that the sons and daughters of such personnel would undoubtedly get an inside track to the jobs by virtue of their parents' location.

In the summer of 1965, the Johnson Administration launched its first Youth Opportunity Campaign. Its purpose was to encourage employers to give summer jobs to needy young people—and the federal government, as the nation's largest employer, was expected to show the way. Participating federal agencies were to hire those people referred to them from the state or local employment service who met the criteria established to define "needy." They were not required to pass any other tests.

The Post Office Department allocated a number of summer jobs to certain post offices as part of the Campaign but notified congressmen of the vacancies and solicited their referrals, insisting that it did so because state and local referral procedures were ineffective. It claimed, too, that it notified all members of Congress, both Republicans and Democrats, but there seems to be confusion on this point. Some Republicans evidently were notified, but others contended that they had not been.

In at least one location, a congressman announced the appointment of individuals just as would be expected if they were appointments to military academies, and one congressman's picture taken with a group of appointees appeared in the newspapers. The press gave the entire situation a thorough review, exposing the fact that, instead of going to the needy, some jobs had gone to sons and daughters of the wealthy and influential as well as to children of postal employees. Commission staff members wanted to disassemble the Post Office Department brick by brick, for the fiasco ended their hope of avoiding nationwide competitive examinations for summer employment.

The House of Representatives, taking note of the happenings, reissued its warning and passed and sent to the Senate the Beckworth bill, which would have required Washington summer jobs to be apportioned fairly among the citizens of all states. The Senate held hearings. The bill appeared headed for passage, but it was allowed to die when the Commission announced that it would hold examinations for the summer of 1966.

Responding to the desire of Congress not to favor Washington residents, the Commission adopted a unique rating procedure. Anyone scoring above 95 could be appointed regardless of where he lived. But no Washington resident with a score below 95 could be appointed as long as candidates were available from outside the area with scores of 95 or above. Through this procedure, the Commission answered both sets of critics—Washington students looking for income and nonresidents looking for broader experience.

The examination proved popular and is still continuing. But it was, and is, as the Commission had anticipated, an expensive undertaking. The simple pamphlet announcing the examination for 1968 cost $35,000 for printing alone. One million copies had to be printed and distributed. The total cost of the examination was $241,000.

The anti-nepotism regulation was modified so that sons and daughters could be hired if their scores in the competitive examination were at least as high as those of other candidates. But the question of hiring the needy still remained. There was clearly social necessity for massive efforts to assure that all young people had opportunity for gainful summer employment. Particular efforts were necessary in behalf of the economically disadvantaged, although this meant departure from the principle of equal opportunity for each opening. The Commission had just suffered a thorough lashing over another kind of favoritism in summer employment, but, in the end, it accepted the rationale that the needy had been deprived of some of the fruits of democracy and could not hope to compete favorably in examinations. Their only opportunity would come from special consideration. The Commission also reasoned that the objectives of the program were so meritorious that, if the hands of greedy politicians could be kept off, the public would understand and accept the Commission's position.

On the whole, the agencies have had good experience with the program. In 1968, some 78,000 disadvantaged youths were employed. There are numerous accounts of school dropouts' returning to the classroom because of new motivation acquired through summer work. There have also been young people inspired to attend college who had never previously entertained such an idea. However, the Commission knows that the Youth Opportunity Program will be watched; if it becomes imbalanced so that other segments of the population feel excluded, there will be new pressures for change.

When Employees Complain

When employees disagree with specific agency policies, there are several avenues open to them. They can employ agency grievance procedures, however inadequate those procedures are. They can write their congressman. They can contact the press. In going outside the agency, they have the obligation to be truthful and not violate agency policies concerning the release of information.

No one has ever given the Commission authority to direct federal agencies in all matters affecting employees. Although the Commission has specific authorities granted to it by executive order and other laws, some authority is given directly to the agencies. Furthermore, the Commission has believed that there are many matters on which agencies should have latitude, and it has delegated as much authority as possible to them. Recently, however, the Commission has been held responsible for things it had earlier considered beyond its purview. This is partly a natural outgrowth of the President's utilization of the Chairman as his personnel adviser. When Congress feels that something in the executive branch needs attention, a Presidential assistant is the logical focal point of pressure. Thus, the Commission has been forced to deal with problems that formerly it would have considered none of its business. Many involve sticky administrative issues.

For example, when Andrews Air Force Base, near Washington, got into financial difficulties and had to lay off some of its custodial force, the management assigned civilian employees, both trade and white-collar workers, to latrine duty. The employees, feeling that they had not been hired for such work, resisted. But resistance in a military organization is trying and often futile. In this instance, they took their grievances to the press, where their case was well publicized.

The Commission had to do something. It conducted a special inspection and found the facts generally as reported, but it also found a politically sensitive issue. The Commission's only authority in the matter related to job classifications. Under the law covering establishment of positions, each job is covered by a written statement of its duties, but it is within the agency's authority to fix the specific duties and the grade in accord with general standards provided by the Commission. The Commission's authority is limited to assuring that standards have been met. Most duty statements describe in detail the primary work to be performed and then close with the meaningful words "performs other duties as assigned." This phrase gives managers the latitude to shift workers to meet workload demands. It had never occurred to anyone that white-collar or skilled trades workers might be given the regular chore of latrine-cleaning.

Although the Commission was expected to do something, there was considerable question as to its authority. The Air Force brass would not be easily intimidated by a soft voice from outside, and the legal subtleties failed to impress the angered employees. After considerable study, the Commission finally instructed all agencies to avoid assigning menial duties inconsistent with those normally performed as a part of the job for which the employee had initially been hired.

Perhaps no personnel problem more delicate than eliminating racial prejudice in employment has ever existed. The Commission has lived in a withering crossfire between people impatient with the rate of social change and people who feel that the rate is too rapid. Although the Civil Service Act prohibits discrimination for reasons of race or religion, the simple fact is that discrimination has occurred. The evidence was clear and unmistakable just by looking at the personnel of offices and establishments not too many years ago. Few Negroes were to be seen performing anything other than menial jobs. Even in the Commission, no Negro was in the higher grades until 1962.

There had been many ways of discriminating without overtly violating the law. Any qualified Negro had to be admitted to an examination, but, if there were too few available in a particular occupational field, such as stenography, agencies could send recruiting teams to high schools. However, since they chose the schools in which they recruited, it was easy for them to select communities in which there were no Negro schools.

Although the problem began to receive attention late in the 1930's, not until the Kennedy and Johnson administrations did it receive real emphasis. Federal managers were then instructed to act, but to them acting meant only one thing: changing the racial ratios at all levels of government employment. Although they felt that the problem could be solved at entrance levels, this alone was not enough. The absence of Negroes from high-grade jobs was embarrassing and offered graphic proof of previous discriminatory practice. Many believed their should be compensation for past errors. In turn, however, the emphasis on hiring and promoting Negroes elicited unhappy reactions from some whites, who claimed that there was now discrimination against them in favor of Negroes.

The Commission, thus, found itself in the middle of one of the most sensitive personnel issues of recent years. It had moved quickly and firmly in the Kennedy Administration to purify the processes over which it had direct control. But, when President Johnson abolished the President's Committee on Equal Employment Opportunity, transferring functions to the Commission, it found itself with a new set of problems. Because many Negroes were distrustful of the "personnel establishment," which they felt allowed discrimination to occur, the Commission had to convince them that it would discharge its new responsibility aggressively. At the same time, it was watched carefully by people who feared that it might be overzealous. It was in this atmosphere that the Commission made a crucial decision, which was to have unfortunate results.

For many years, no one had been satisfied with the statistics on the racial composition of the federal workforce or with the method of gathering them. Prohibitions against asking questions about race and religion on applications and against recording such information on personnel records had long been in effect, for obvious reasons—if the race and religion of a person are unknown, neither can be a factor in selection. At the same time, however, it was necessary to know the racial composition to determine the racial balance within the government. The only way the composition could be determined was by a periodic head count by supervisors. Minority group representatives disliked this method, which they felt was undignified and of questionable accuracy. After discussion with agency employees and personnel officials, the Commission concluded that the best way to obtain the needed information was by a direct but voluntary questionnaire to the employees, provided that the information would be kept out of agency personnel records. That no one would be required to respond to the questionnaire was stressed.

The reaction was totally unexpected. Although it had been feared that Negroes would distrust the questionnaire, the reverse happened. There had been so much publicity concerning the emphasis on Negro employment opportunity that some white employees reacted strongly. Members of one group in New York all indicated that they were American Indians. The dissatisfaction was so widespread and intense that the Commission had to abandon the questionnaire and go back to a head count. But the problems were not over.

Many employees wrote to Congress with complaints about all the policies that bothered them. Although several congressional committees previously had been interested in some of the matters employees wrote about, the Senate Subcommittee on Constitutional Rights became interested in all of them. It felt that the individual rights of employees were being violated.

Complaints varied widely. Some originated strictly within the employees' own agencies; others were the result of Commission administered policies. Employees wrote, for example, of the campaign to encourage them to purchase savings bonds through the payroll deduction plan, which had been conducted with such vigor in some agencies, particularly in the Post Office Department, that they felt coerced to buy, whether or not they could afford to or wanted to. They wrote of the efforts of the executive branch to solve the problem of conflict of interest, which had plagued past administrations. To guard against this problem, the Johnson Administration had issued a set of ground rules for ethical conduct, which many employees found objectionable, and the Commission was made responsible for administering the regulations. A key requirement was that employees in a position to influence policy or business items such as awarding of contracts should disclose their financial holdings. Some agencies interpreted the Commission's instructions far too literally and applied them to ridiculous extremes. The Smithsonian Institution, for instance, required employees at the clerical level to file statements of their financial status.

Some employees wrote of agency promotion procedures that they considered irrelevant or offensive. The Commission had long permitted agencies to apply stricter or higher standards for internal promotions than for recruitment from outside the service. In many instances, agencies used written tests not required by the Commission. For some particularly sensitive jobs, they used personality tests containing very personal questions, which, on the surface at least, appeared to be of questionable relevance. In addition, medical questionnaires used in physical examinations contained questions considered offensive to employees. The complaints added up to a feeling that federal employees were the victims of unwarranted invasions of privacy.

As publicity mounted, more items were brought to the attention of the Senate Committee. The Commission investigated all of them and found some surprises. It learned that employees of one agency were not permitted access to their personnel office. It found medical questionnaire forms still in use that it had declared obsolete many years previously. As each practice was spotlighted, the Commission was looked to as the agent of the executive branch that could and should do something about it.

With personality or psychological testing, the Commission

was in difficulty. It had long ago learned to be extremely careful about questions on all its examinations, and it had banned
the use of personality questions whenever its authority to do so
was clear. This task was not always easy. For example, the
Federal Aviation Agency (now the Federal Aviation Administration) employed special tests for certain highly responsible air-traffic control work. After some study, the
Commission required a modification, but there were several
interagency encounters before the FAA was willing to accept
the decision.

The Senate was impressed with the complaints of employees.
After hearings attended by much publicity, it passed and sent
to the House, in September, 1967, a bill that became known
as the Employee Bill of Rights. The bill would have prohibited a wide range of official activity considered to be an
unwarranted invasion of employee privacy, such as inquiry
concerning race, religion, and national origin, coercion to buy
savings bonds, use of medical questionnaires and certain forms
of psychological testing, and use of lie-detectors to determine
sexual attitudes, except in clearly defined limited circumstances. The bill also covered applicants as well as employees.
The bill would have established an independent bipartisan
board of three members, appointed by the President with the
consent of the Senate, to administer the new program. It would
have permitted employees to appear directly to the board or to
take their grievances into the federal district courts.

The Commission vigorously opposed the bill. It felt that
establishing an appeal procedure in addition to what it considered already comprehensive grievance procedures and
setting forth in law rights of employees without balancing
them with a statement of employee obligations would make a
shambles of federal personnel management. Further, the board
would have part of the functions currently allocated to the
Commission, and confusion would undoubtedly result.

The Commission argued that the objectives of the bill could
better be achieved by executive action through existing

agencies. Although the Commission had investigated numerous complaints and found them to be valid, it felt certain that they were extreme and unusual rather than examples of widespread practice. Furthermore, action had been taken to put an end to each bad practice as it had been identified.

The bill passed the Senate by an overwhelming majority. The Subcommittee on Manpower and Civil Service of the House Post Office and Civil Service Committee held hearings but seemed much less concerned over the matter than the Senate, and the bill was allowed to die in committee.

This episode grew out of a complex combination of actions and inactions, some misinterpreted. The Commission's race questionnaire was designed to improve efficiency, but its intention was misunderstood. Other actions pointed up the need for central agency attention to issues over which the Commission previously had felt it had no authority or to problems it had assumed would be handled properly by any manager with good judgment. What happened demonstrated to the Commission that formal appeals and grievance procedures do not provide an adequate channel for large numbers of public employees to voice their discontent and that a group believing itself to be unfairly used will find articulate spokesmen. Since, in this case, the only channels open to them outside the agencies were the press and Congress, the employees availed themselves of those.

In response, the Commission established the Office of Civil Service Complaints to report to the executive director. While directed toward employee interests, it also receives complaints about the civil service system from employees, applicants, or the public at large. Its function is to see that the complaints are reviewed by the appropriate office of the Commission or agency and that the complaint is given a timely answer. A more fundamental purpose, however, is to give the Commission the opportunity to identify problem areas as they develop so that early corrective action may be taken.

Although the office is new, the idea of establishing it was

not. The Commission had previously considered setting up such an office, but its involvement with many items seemingly of higher priority had caused the idea to be shelved. The malpractices exposed and the reaction of the Senate, undoubtedly, led to a re-evaluation of priorities.

QUALITY AND INEQUALITY

Before 1962, the Commission's principle concern in filling jobs was to recruit the best-qualified persons obtainable. "Quest for quality" was its recruiting slogan, usually interpreted to mean searching for the person with the most success to his credit—either in experence or in education, sometimes in both. The slogan was broadcast far and wide and introduced into every Commission brochure.

When employment began to be looked upon as a key to solving social problems, however, the question was asked: "What has become of the quest for quality?" The Commission's answer was simple. The quest for quality had never meant seeking overqualified people; it had meant seeking the best-qualified under a given set of circumstances.

The Commission had rather dramatic evidence to support its view. When a campaign to employ the mentally retarded was inaugurated in 1963, many people were skeptical, but those who "came to scoff remained to praise." The mentally retarded, carefully evaluated and trained and well placed, actually performed certain routine jobs better than the unhandicapped.

When the Commission undertook a special program for summer employment of economically disadvantaged youth, many people felt that the Commission had taken an inconsistent position.

What gave rise to this feeling was probably the number of special emphasis programs being planned simultaneously. When women complained of discrimination, a womanpower program was launched; when Negroes and other minority groups spoke, the drive to eliminate all vestiges of discrimination intensified. The program to hire economically disadvantaged young people in the summer fell into this category, as did a special activity to give work to prisoners whose terms were soon to be up and who were considered good employment risks.

Personnel officers and agency heads were asked to push each program with equal force, which unquestionably brought frustration and encouraged needling comments. To such questions as "Which programs should have priority?" and "How do I reconcile hiring prisoners and marginally qualified hardcore unemployed from the ghetto with the quest for quality?" the Commissioner's answer was that all the programs were important and none were inconsistent with the objectives of seeking the best-qualified person for each job.

A problem inherent in the traditional approach was uncovered by the Subcommittee on Manpower and Civil Service of the House Post Office and Civil Service Committee. A high-ranking officer who had retired from military service was seeking an appointment for the lowest-grade job in civil service. After competing in an examination, he was appointed and, shortly thereafter, promoted. Under traditional interpretations and procedures, the officer could obviously do better than his competitors, who had only minimal qualifications. As a result, they would be shut off from the opportunity to work at the only level for which they were qualified. The problem faced by the Commission was how to modify its traditional interpretation of qualifications and testing procedures. Education beyond the ability to read and write is not required for many jobs. In many instances, the qualities needed are motivation, willingness, ability to follow instructions, contentment with routine and repetitive tasks, and physical strength and endurance.

The Commission solved the problem with an examination that departs from the traditional practice of giving weight to experience and education. Under the new tests, an obviously overqualified person might wind up lower on the list than one with a much less substantial background.

Federal employment policies have traditionally protected the public interest and the reputation of the government service. Doubts about an applicant's character and suitability were resolved in favor of the government. The maxim of appointing officers was "don't knowingly buy a risk." Consequently, many people were not hired because of information on their job applications, even though the Commission's suitability standards might have permitted their employment.

For example, all applicants were asked whether they had ever been arrested and convicted for anything other than minor traffic offenses. Those concerned with ghetto problems contended that the question was improper, that many of the people they were trying to help had arrest records that were relatively meaningless. The Commission changed its question to inquire about convictions, not arrests.

The entire thrust of those attacking the problems of unemployment and poverty was that employers would have to begin to take risks with marginal applicants. The federal government, the nation's largest employer, was expected to set the example. It was something of a wrench for employees used to devising procedures for keeping out marginal job-seekers now to encourage their employment under certain conditions.

But in this, as in many areas, the Commission recognized that the circumstances were such as to require new approaches. Adjustments were made. Time alone can prove their wisdom.

IX

The Commission and Congress

Like all other agencies, the Commission's success depends on the good will of Congress. To every federal agency, Congress is the giver of life and the potential speller of doom. Congress deals in wants. It does not always get what it wants, but, usually, what it does not want, nobody gets. Annually, all agencies want money to accomplish their mission; Congress appropriates the money. In this respect, the Commission's relationships with Congress are no different from those of other agencies.

In theory, the annual appropriation request reflects the amount of money the executive branch feels is necessary to carry out the programs the American people have assigned to it through laws enacted by Congress. The only real basis for argument is price—how much something should cost. Of course, this is an oversimplification, for laws passed by Congress are naturally very broad, and agencies have much latitude for action under them. Consequently, it is possible to engage in activities that Congress did not originally envision. The annual appropriation process gives Congress the opportunity to touch base—to review agencies' operation and to approve or disapprove as it chooses.

Beyond the annual appropriation, agencies have other wants that they must take to Congress to satisfy. They frequently need legislation to carry out new programs that they determine to be in the public interest and they sometimes feel they need new or expanded authority to improve an existing function. In such circumstances, agencies clearly need friends on Capitol Hill; they can afford few enemies. Therefore, whenever a senator or member of the House of Representatives asks a question of an agency official, it receives the highest priority. If possible and proper, a congressional request is honored; if not, a careful and friendly explanation is made.

Although the Commission shares the common denominator of dependence upon Congressional good will with all executive-branch agencies, its relationships with Capitol Hill have many unique aspects. Most departments and agencies have special constituencies to serve. For instance, the Department of Labor deals with problems of specific concern to particularly defined groups of people and it designs and administers programs in their interest. The Commission has wide public contact, but it is primarily concerned with internal management of the executive branch. What it does affects every department and agency and brings it into contact at one time or another with almost every committee of Congress. In the 90th Congress, for instance, the Commission was required to submit reports on 500 bills. Seventeen House committees and fourteen Senate committees were involved. Testimony was required at fifty-four hearings. These proceedings, of course, do not include the activity and hearings involved in the Commission's annual appropriation requests.

Even though the Commission has much congressional business, much of its work is not a bread-and-butter item to a member of Congress. His primary concerns are likely to be the things that are of greatest interest to his constituents, possibly local problems, taxes, the cost of living, or social or international issues, not, usually, personnel management. In itself, personnel management is not sufficienty tangible to arouse his interest. It encompasses so many different things that it has to be broken down into specific items, some of great interest but others unlikely to excite enthusiasm. For instance, if the

Commission is dealing with the pay of employees, congressional interest and attention is easily gained. Pay has two features that bring automatic congressional interest: its effect on the federal worker who can pressure Congress through union activity and its effect on the enormous federal payroll, which is of concern to every taxpayer. However, if the Commission seeks congressional approval of an item primarily of agency management interest, such as authority to establish 300 more top positions, it may have difficulty gaining attention.

The Commission is not a major contributor to the congressman's solution of the problems of his constituents. It does not build dams; it does not construct large government facilities. It has no commodity for which a member of Congress and his constituency feel a specific need. But it does have great influence on how jobs are obtained. Here, unfortunately, its function, in the eyes of the congressman, is more likely to be negative than positive. When a constituent wants the assistance of a member of Congress in getting a federal job, the Commission is more likely to be considered the problem than the answer. As a result, a congressman or senator may be inclined to remember the Commission more for the things it does not do than for the things it does.

Congress Wants a Watchdog

The General Accounting Office is a congressional agent responsible for policing the financial stewardship of the executive branch. In many ways, Congress, particularly the Post Office and Civil Service committees, appears to desire, if not expect, the same kind of policing from the Commission in personnel administration throughout government. Yet, the relationships are entirely different. The General Accounting Office is a part of the legislative branch and the Civil Service Law clearly places the Commission under the President. Until recently, the Commission has generally made certain that it has carried out its assigned duties but has not gone into other areas unless certain that its actions would accord with the desires of the President or would be required by law. This philosophy has not always met congressional acclaim. Consequently, at times when the Commission has been least aggressive or when its authority to act has been unclear, it has literally been picked up by the scruff of the neck and thrown into action by Congress.

Whenever Congress is displeased or wants action not coming from the executive branch, it legislates. The executive branch wants legislation in the form of authority to act, but it also wants flexibility to exercise that authority. It hates administration by legislation. When a detail of administration is written into law, often latitude for reasonable adjustment to meet varying conditions disappear.

When members of the House Appropriations Committee were unhappy because the Commission had approved maximum age limits for certain job categories, they proposed legislation that, when enacted, prohibited the Commission from setting any such limitations for any job, even for an apprentice trainee. In this instance, Congress inserted a few words in the Commission's annual appropriation language. The law now simply reads: "Appropriated funds may not be used to pay an employee who establishes a maximum age requirement for entrance into the competitive service." The wording represents an interesting and effective technique. It does not say there can be no age limits. It merely says that an employee who establishes one cannot have his salary paid with appropriated funds. However, since employees of the Commission who set standards like to be paid for their work, there are no maximum age limits.

Sometimes the threat of legislation is enough to cause the executive branch to act. It was largely to avoid legislation that the Commission moved into the merit promotion system in the 1950's. Likewise, the threat of legislation forced the Commission to adopt the nationwide summer employment examination in 1965.

In several instances, Congress has made it necessary for the Commission to apply controls to agency actions, sometimes against the Commission's own desires. By requiring it to review and approve appointments to supergrade positions in both the competitive and excepted services, Congress put the Commission in an area that had been considered off limits. Indeed, the Commission had believed that the reason for excepting a position from the competitive examining requirements was to give the agency head the opportunity to determine and apply his own qualification standards in filling jobs.

When Congress became concerned about military personnel retiring to enter civil service, it required the Commission to review and approve individual personnel transactions that normally would have been considered within the province of the Department of Defense. Sometimes the line between work performed by military and civilian personnel is very blurred, and it was not uncommon for persons retiring from the military to be retained in civilian capacities to perform exactly the same duties as those he performed in uniform. This practice was dubbed by the House Post Office and Civil Service Committee as a "buddy" system, because one member of the armed forces got another to put aside a civilian job for him when he took off the uniform. Feeling unable to get the Department of Defense to stop the practice by administrative action, the committee sponsored and gained enactment of special legislation. The law prohibited a member of the armed forces from taking a civilian position anywhere in the Department of Defense within 180 days following retirement, unless certain specified conditions were met, including approval by the Commission. In fact, Congress was requiring the Commission to police a law directed toward the actions of a specific agency, a position the Commission has not always been happy to take.

The Commission's relationship with Congress, however, has not always been guided by an iron hand from Capitol Hill. The Subcommittee on Manpower and Civil Service of the

House Post Office and Civil Service Committee has been particularly aggressive in drawing the Commission into situations it might otherwise have left to agency management. The Committee's staff members travel widely and visit many federal employees at all levels. They frequently report findings to the Commission, which may make a special inspection and, depending on its own findings, order corrective action or make policy or procedural adjustments, whichever is appropriate. There is nothing in the law requiring the committee staff to work in this way with the Commission, but the fact that they do is evidence of the rapport between the two bodies in recent years.

Sometimes Congress finds a simple and direct solution to a problem that the Commission had been unsuccessful in settling. One such problem, nagging to the Commission and to all administrators of merit systems, concerns temporary appointment to a job for which there is no open examination or current list of eligibles at the time the vacancy occurs. Obviously the work has to be done, and an agency cannot be expected to delay its work and wait a long time for a list of examination eligibles. Sometimes because of workload, lack of resources, or both, it is impossible to conduct an examination immediately. The Commission's standard procedure is to allow the agency to recruit someone on a temporary basis who meets the qualification requirements. In many state and local civil service jurisdictions, these appointments are called "provisional." In the federal service, they are called "TAPERS," derived from "temporary appointment pending establishment of register." The person holding such an appointment is known as a TAPER.

In theory, TAPERS would stay in the job until an examination was held, with continued occupancy subject to passing the examination with a score high enough to make appointment from the register possible. In practice, however, TAPERS stayed on the rolls for several years, without, of course, the full benefits of tenure. The examining program was never able to take care of them all. Every few years, executive orders blanketed them into the service noncompetitively.

The Commission had debated the matter for years. Some staff members believed that there should be a rule established by executive order to permit the noncompetitive conversion of any TAPER appointee after a specified time, perhaps three years, if no appropriate examination were held. Thus, temporary appointees would acquire the same rights as employees of the legislative branch who likewise had taken no competitive examination. Others felt that this conversion would provide a back-door entry into the service that would cushion the examining system from pressure to maintain current lists of eligibles.

Although the Commission found that there were approximately 5,000 persons throughout the service holding TAPER appointments, agencies generally did not seem overly concerned. The Department of Defense had the largest bloc, but this seemed not to alarm them.

The problem came under congressional review when a few employees in the Federal Maritime Commission, one of the smaller agencies, brought it to the attention of the Senate Post Office and Civil Service Committee. They had taken their plight to the Commission previously but had received only the word that theirs was part of a much larger problem that was being worked on. The Senate committee staff members called the Commission and got much the same response. After a short while, the committee tired of waiting on the Commission, and Senator A. S. Mike Monroney introduced a bill to permit TAPER employees noncompetitive conversion to career status upon the recommendation of the employing agency after three years of satisfactory service. After considerable examination of the problem, the Commission supported the legislation, and a satisfactory bill became law.

It is interesting that the Commission had been aware of the problem for many years but was fearful that the course of action eventually taken would be controversial and probably open to political attack by those who would see in it the possibility of the party in power giving tenure to persons who had not been appointed from competitive examinations. The Commission also feared that this conversion plan would make the system more vulnerable to the machinations of anyone with both the power and the desire to circumvent the merit system by expanding direct appointments and curtailing the examining program.

Congress saw the temporary appointment system as an injustice to the employees, however, and the legislation, while it was under consideration, encountered no serious opposition and no public clamor. It is probable, however, that had the executive branch initiated the action, the Commission would have been looked upon with suspicion and public debate would have ensued.

LINES OF COMMUNICATION

Communications between the Commission and Congress range from a published annual report of the Commission's activity, required by law, to informal, day-in-day-out contact with individual members of Congress and committee staffs. Many agencies maintain a special staff whose responsibility is to handle any problem or question raised by a member of Congress. In recent years, the Commission has preferred to discontinue this practice. It maintains the Civil Service Information Office in the Rayburn Building on the "House side" of Capitol Hill to provide the members or their visiting constituents with information about federal job opportunities, but substantive questions are referred to the appropriate Commission office. It has been Commission doctrine that each key staff member should be prepared to explain his particular operation and handle problems arising within it. A special liaison staff would only be an unnecessary layer.

Commission staff members do not initiate formal contacts

with members of Congress except in the most unusual circumstances or when asked to do so by the Chairman or one of the other commissioners. There is, however, frequent informal contact initiated by the Commission with committee staff personnel or key members of the Senate or House to consult on specific problems. When a new program of any significance is launched, even though it may be fully within the Commission's authority to proceed, Commission representatives normally try to brief them or to at least get their reactions. If there is little or no reaction, the program proceeds; if it appears that Congress will be displeased, a careful review is made before going ahead. Sometimes consultations merely take soundings before a plan is developed. Many ideas have been scuttled on the drawing board as a result of informal conversations.

Realizing that members of Congress have many problems involving the Commission, every effort is made to provide them with information to aid their constituents. In cooperation with the Post Office and Civil Service committees of the House and Senate, the Commission conducts special briefing services for new members or their administrative assistants early in each new Congress. The objective is to inform them of Commission activities and services. Whether or not such sessions are held and whether they are attended is, of course, up to Congress. The Commission likes the plan, which has met with moderate success, for it believes that the more understanding the members and their staffs have about various programs, the better everyone will be served. In the sessions, key members of the Commission staff working with matters most likely to be of interest to Congress are introduced and the activities for which they are responsible are explained. The hope is that, when the congressional office encounters a problem, it will know where to direct its inquiry.

Every American citizen can write to his elected representative for assistance in dealing with one of the federal agencies. If the problem concerns agriculture, he may want his representative in Congress to intercede with the Department of Agriculture; if it concerns a federal job, there is a good chance the problem may involve the Commission.

Under the Civil Service Law, persons involved in conducting examinations or making appointments may not receive or consider recommendations from a member of Congress concerning an applicant except those relating "to the character or residence of the applicant." This fact, however, in no way keeps citizens from seeking the assistance of Congress. There is still a feeling on the part of many people that political influence helps.

Members of Congress handle requests for assistance in getting jobs in different ways. Some of the longtime members have decided that it is best to advise constituents of the existence of the merit system and that intercession by them would be both improper and a waste of time; therefore, they rarely write to the Commission. Others believe that they should demonstrate interest in the applicant by writing to or calling the Commission, indicating the applicant's interest and inquiring of the Commission concerning his prospects for appointment.

The Commission, realizing the congressman's problem, replies to his request by writing a letter that explains how the merit system works, even though it may have explained the same thing a hundred times previously. This procedure saves the congressman's office the trouble of composing technical responses. Often, the congressman merely sends a copy of the Commission's reply to the constituent. By so doing, the congressman can let his constituent know that he has performed a service in his behalf and, at the same time, place responsibility on the agency that may be giving an answer the constituent does not wish to hear.

If the constituent's inquiry is about job opportunities in a specific field, the Commission supplies information concerning the appropriate examination and on how to apply. If it concerns someone who has taken and passed an examination and is on the list of eligibles, the Commission sends what is known internally as the "prospects letter." The Commission looks at the applicant's score and position on the list in relation to the number of jobs being filled and makes a conservative estimate of his prospects for consideration by an employing agency in the near future. An appraisal of "excellent" means that the candidate is within reach for certification and that a certificate is expected to be issued very shortly. "Very good" means that he will undoubtedly be certified before too many weeks if the job placement volume holds up. Appraisals "fair" and "poor" mean that the candidate's score is low and certification is unlikely. Being high enough on a list to be certified to an agency is by no means assurance of a job. The agency has the right to appoint or not appoint as its judgment dictates, and the Commission's letter usually stresses this fact.

Of course, not all the problems raised with a member of Congress by his constituents have to do with assistance in obtaining a job. Issues may cover any aspect of federal employment, including questions about a particular program, complaints about the handling of a specific case, pleas for help from an applicant who has been rated ineligible or a federal employee who feels he has been unfairly treated.

The Commission reads its congressional mail closely to identify what needs attention. Sometimes it spots problems that were not the basis of the inquiry. Rather than being resentful of the inquiries, the Commission has come to look upon them as valuable indicators of how things are actually working. Many revisions in programs and policies stem from questions posed by persons writing to members of Congress. In fact, the major overhaul of the civil service examining program and the creation of the sixty-five coordinated interagency boards of examiners was in part attributed to questions raised by congressional constituents, which convinced the Commission that the system had to be simplified for public convenience. The original system was almost impossible for the experts to explain, let alone the general public to understand (see Chapter III). Complaints were most often about specific situations, whose origins, the Commission found, stemmed from the complex manner in which the examining program was carried out.

Another policy revision grew out of a complaint forwarded by a member of Congress concerning a constituent who, at the request of agencies, had made extended trips to be interviewed for employment. The constituent's primary complaint was about the treatment he had received at the interviews. Although his reception was of concern to the Commission, that the agency had neglected to heed a long-standing prohibition against requiring persons to travel unreasonable distances to be interviewed was of greater concern. If an agency chose to hold prehiring interviews, its responsibility was to have an interviewer within reasonable distance of the applicant. Until this congressional query and a few more like it were made, the Commission was unaware that the policy was being ignored. The Commission subsequently tightened up its instructions to agencies.

THE WORKING ARENA

Any box score of Commission-Congress relations viewed from the vantage of the Commission would reflect successes as well as failures. The pay-reform legislation of the 1960's would have to be scored as a spectacular success. The Employee Bill of Rights, which passed the Senate, but never reached the House floor for vote (see Chapter VIII), must be considered a setback. The Commission could not persuade the Congress of its own desire, or its capability, to protect satisfactorily the rights of employees.

In recent years, the Commission's staff has worked closely with congressional committees to effect a number of noteworthy achievements. The Commission has staff members who are experts in the fields of retirement, life and health insurance, pay, and personnel security. They often work as consultants to legislative committees, help to draft legislation, with the understanding that the Commission is institutionally not necessarily committed to any particular position. Whenever a major piece of personnel legislation moves through Congress, it is almost always safe to conclude that staff members of the Commission and the appropriate legislative committees are red-eyed from loss of sleep and are viewing the entire process with detached academic interest, while their respective bosses may be slugging it out to achieve different objectives.

It is not at all uncommon for the Commission officially to oppose legislation that one of its staff members has helped draft. This is thoroughly understood by all parties and is good testimony to the high regard in which the Commission staff members are held. So good is their reputation for objectivity that they have been known to write the minority and the majority reports on the same bill if there were such marked division of opinion that the minority wished to have its position stated. The experienced staff man, whether in the legislative or the executive branch, is able to view both sides of a controversial issue, particularly one in which partisan politics is involved.

The posture of the executive and legislative branches and the art of political maneuver is generally the same, regardless of which party is in power. What one veteran career official said of another who retired shortly after the Kennedy Administration took office is called to mind: "He's been through the Roosevelt New Deal, the Truman Fair Deal, the Eisenhower Great Crusade, and now the Kennedy New Frontier, and they all look alike to him."

SUPERGRADES AND SUPER HEADACHES

An area of almost constant negotiation between the Commission and Congress involves the establishment of the so-called supergrades in the federal government. Its discussion requires some historical setting. The story is complex and undergirded with the kind of legislative inconsistency that is sometimes the hallmark of democracy. In 1949, when Congress passed a new position classification act covering the grading of most white-collar positions, it authorized three new grades on top of the previous schedule. The top position under the old law had been Grade 15; the new top was Grade 18, with intervening Grades 16 and 17. These new grades naturally carried higher rates of pay than any authorized by the previous law. The executive branch persuaded Congress to authorize the jobs by explaining that they were needed to ensure that the federal service could recruit badly needed talent.

The new jobs were immediately tagged with the name "supergrades," and therein may have been the beginning of difficulty. They continued to be looked upon as something unique, requiring special controls. Because they were new and represented liberalization, the executive branch was not given unlimited license to establish them. Congress kept control by placing a ceiling of 400 on the number of such jobs that could be established; there are no ceiling controls at Grade 15 and below.

Congress gave the Commission the thankless job of determining which of the many agency jobs merited allocation to the new grades. Each agency quite naturally felt that many of its jobs deserved the new grades, but there were not enough supergrades to go around. Although the original ceiling of 400 has now been greatly raised, the Commission has always felt that the rigid congressional control does not permit the executive branch the flexibility it needs.

Not long after the law was passed, Congress complicated the Commission's position and created problems from which the system has never fully recovered by authorizing specific agencies to place certain jobs at the supergrade level over and above the ceiling. These authorizations were made almost on a hit-or-miss basis as specific agency programs were reviewed by congressional committees. This practice has ceased, but the Commission was left with some jobs allocated to the supergrades that it felt were of lower priority than some in other agencies. Because of the ceiling, the Commission could not approve additional supergrades for the jobs it believed were more deserving. Agencies increased their pressure on the Commission as these inequities occurred, but the Commission could only draw the problem to the attention of Congress.

In 1962, the ceiling was completely lifted on research jobs in science and engineering approved by the Commission, but it was retained for jobs in other categories. Because of growth and changes in government structure, the Commission always has a backlog of cases for which agencies have properly recommended supergrades but on which it has been hamstrung by the ceilings and unable to make assignments. The net effect is some unavoidable inequity between agencies and even within agencies. In testimony before the Senate Post Office and Civil Service Committee in March, 1968, Chairman Macy pointed out that half of the regional directors of the National Labor Relations Board were GS-16 and half were GS-15.

An additional headache for the Commission was the fact that it had to approve not only jobs but individuals in the supergrade category. Late in the 1950's, Congress had granted an executive-branch request to enlarge the supergrade ceiling but coupled it with a requirement that, in the future, any appointments to the jobs, with certain specified exceptions, must have the Commission's approval. This meant that even positions not subject to competitive examining requirements at the policy-making level, where political considerations might enter into the selection, must be reviewed. Congress needed some safeguards to ensure that its objectives in authorizing the jobs were being met, that these new grades were aiding the recruitment and retention of high-quality personnel.

The problem of establishing supergrades and approving appointments to those jobs has placed the Commission in a difficult position. It must represent the needs of the executive branch and at the same time apply the restraints required by Congress. The Johnson Administration, for instance, requested authority from the 90th Congress for 245 additional supergrades to staff new and expanding programs designed to solve some of the most pressing problems of the day, plus a pool of 100 jobs to be distributed by the Commission to meet other needs. Some of the specific programs were created by congressional actions; others, by executive order. Common to both was the urgent need for executive talent to develop them. But, faced with spiraling costs, inflation, and a bill to increase taxes in an election year, Congress did not buy the Administration's proposal, and the Commission was left with the problem of meeting the demands of agency heads with an empty cupboard.

UNIFORM PERSONNEL POLICY

A problem shared jointly by the Post Office and Civil Service committees and the Commission is keeping personnel laws uniform so that one group of employees does not obtain benefits not enjoyed by all whose conditions of employment are similar.

For the most part, Congress has provided uniform legislation through such laws as the Civil Service Act and those covering leave, job classification, pay, and retirement. However, it must be remembered that, although a single executive can apply controls to assure uniformity of the policy that he determines, no such control is possible in Congress, where policy is made by majority vote. Different groups sometimes apply pressures that are difficult for the legislators to withstand.

The various agency requests and programs are reviewed by different committees with differing interests and objectives. It is not uncommon for legislation to be enacted that makes a special concession to a single agency. Many times, it is legislation the executive branch does not want. Although the individual agency might desire the legislation, it could never officially recommend it, because the Bureau of the Budget must review legislative proposals for conformance to the President's program. The President can control what is recommended. However, no satisfactory way has ever been found to keep Congress from finding out what an agency wants. It can ask questions and proceed to legislate even if the executive branch is opposed. Of course, the President can always veto a law, but sometimes the item in question will be submerged in a piece of major legislation and, although distasteful, will be considered so minor in relation to the total bill that the strategists will conclude that the price of the veto will be greater than the problems created by the law.

A few years ago, the Commission was trying to get Congress to enact legislation to liberalize the payment of moving expenses for federal employees who were transferred to new locations. Under existing law, the amount an employee could be reimbursed did not even begin to cover his expenses. Agencies wanted to encourage the mobility of employees, because, in many instances, it was the best way to provide training for high-grade jobs and it certainly was the best way to fill many vacancies. Many federal managers were reluctant to use their transfer authority because of the financial sacrifice imposed upon the employee.

While the Commission and the House Post Office and Civil Service Committee were working on legislation covering the entire federal service, it was learned that the House Armed Services Committee had added a liberal authority to a piece of Department of Defense legislation that had passed without ever having been referred to the Commission. The Post Office Department was given a similar authority. These two Departments may, under certain circumstances, treat their employees in a way different from the way the rest of the federal service treats employees. Such double standards are almost bound to bring future difficulties to both Congress and the Commission.

Another interesting action illustrates this problem. Over the Commission's vigorous opposition, the 90th Congress passed legislation that gave the entire federal fringe-benefits package, including retirement, to Agricultural Conservation Service employees in the states. Though these employees are paid from federal funds granted to the states, the Commission contends that they are employees of the state, not the federal government. What makes this arrangement particularly difficult is the fact that there are now many state and local programs funded by federal money, and the Commission feels that the action of Congress concerning the one group of employees may have opened a barrel of inconsistencies.

Many years ago, the FBI convinced Congress that, because of hazardous duty, its agents should be able to retire after twenty years of service. Other law-enforcement officers, such as the narcotics agents of the Treasury, did not enjoy similar privileges, yet they had some of the most dangerous assignments imaginable. Although this inequity was taken care of in time, until additional legislation could be obtained it presented major headaches. But the early-retirement controversy has not ended. The air-traffic controllers of the Federal Aviation Administration have been trying for some years to make the case that they, too, should be permitted early retirement because of the pressure and tension under which they work. They of course cannot make the point of physical danger, but they can raise the question of the impact on the safety of the traveling public when controllers remain on the the job beyond the time when they can be expected to be at their peak of physical and mental capacity. The Commission and the Congress face a difficult question, as yet unanswered.

POSTMASTERS, RURAL CARRIERS, THE COMMISSIONS, AND CONGRESS

The appointment of postmasters and rural letter carriers has provided much contact between the Commission and individual members of Congress as well as with the Senate Post Office and Civil Service Committee. Many families are saddled with a relative they would prefer to disclaim but who always shows up to dominate the annual reunion; so has it been with the Commission and the postmaster- and rural-carrier problem. The Commission would like to ignore the existence of such a defective employment apparatus within its domain, but it cannot, and it has almost despaired of trying to reform it.

Real reform requires two ingredients: willingness to crusade on the part of the President and action by Congress. Until the announcement by President Nixon (see page 64), both had been absent. In many instances, congressmen belonging to the party in power have made the actual appointments.

The strange part is that, although postmaster appointments are covered by separate law, rural carrier appointments are under the Civil Service Act. Therefore, the adviser system is as illegal for rural carriers as it would be for any other job covered by the competitive service, but it has been tolerated nonetheless. If the practice were made in other jobs in the competitive service, heads would surely roll.

Through the years, the problem of these postal positions has been very discomforting to the Commission, which, powerless to eliminate the situation, has generally ignored it or spoken about it in hushed tones. To the Bureau of Recruiting and Examining, this has been amusing, for its staff members have been in daily contact with the realities. They have received innumerable calls from members of Congress, for whom there is no doubt about the processes of selection, as well as directly from county committeemen.

The Johnson Administration initiated the first moves in many years toward a total clean-up of the situation. The tactic was not to strike out with a forceful act of internal orders on rural carriers and a formal proposal of legislation on postmasters. Instead it was to gain support for change through the art of "reasoning together." Contacts were made with key members of the Senate and the House. It was thought that, if Congress would agree to change the law on post-masters, rural carriers could then easily be taken care of by the executive branch. For a time it appeared that this approach might work. Senator A. S. "Mike" Monroney sponsored legis-lation that would have eliminated Senate confirmation of post-masters and placed the position in the same category as any other job. It passed the Senate, but it was hopelessly buried in committee when the 90th Congress adjourned. Congressman Arnold Olsen of Montana also introduced a bill in the House with similar objectives. It was reported favorably by the Post Office and Civil Service Committee, but it too died with con-gressional adjournment.

President Nixon's move to eliminate politics from the selec-tion process was both dramatic and politically courageous. It remains to be seen how effectively his wishes will be carried out, for individual members of Congress will still be under heavy pressure to assist constituents who want jobs.

THE DESIGNATION EXAMINATION: A SPECIAL SERVICE TO CONGRESS

A little-publicized but long-established activity of the Com-mission places it in a unique relation to individual members of Congress. Although members of Congress designate persons for appointment to the military academies, the candidates still must pass the entrance examinations of the specific academies. Congressmen and senators frequently have many more young men who desire appointments than there are openings and want to be relatively certain that their candi-dates will be admitted. As a service to Congress, the Commis-sion conducts an examination twice a year or more fre-quently, if necessary. The examination does not count for anything more than the member of Congress wishes. It is specifically designed to predict the candidate's ability to pass the official academy entrance examination at a later date should he be selected to take it. There is no requirement that the members of Congress use the examination (and not all of them do), but many use it as a guide in making their selections.

The Commission announces the date and location of the examination and asks congressmen to submit, by a specified date, the names and locations of their applicants. It then administers the tests, scores the papers, and turns the results over to the congressman to use as he chooses. It is all done on a very tight schedule.

The entire operation is routine, but it involves extremely sensitive relationships between the staffs of the Commission and the members of Congress. It is conducted largely by experienced clerks who know how to get things done under the tension of short deadlines. They handle calmly and without panic many incidents that often make the high-level executives shake their heads and cross their fingers when they think about the possibility of errors and their consequences.

Although each congressional office is given a "deadline" for submitting names so the Commission will know how many candidates have to be tested and where, if a congressional office calls at the last minute and wants a young man admitted to the test, it is considered advisable to accommodate him. The Commission plans for such contingencies, which occur frequently.

Because the examination involves so many people at so many locations, the margin for trouble is wide. There have been a few incidents that have caused nerves to fray but none that have not been handled quietly. Usually, whenever congressional offices have understood the problem, they have been particularly sympathetic.

A few years ago, the entire set of tests from one examining point disappeared in the mail. They were mailed by the examiner at the conclusion of the test but never arrived in the Commission. Since the papers were thought to be lost in the mail, the Post Office became involved. Postal inspectors conducted an exhaustive search for the missing tests, but without success. Experienced Commission personnel were suspicious that the package had been delivered and, through some horrible miscalculation, had been placed with obsolete test questions headed for the official incinerator, but—fortunately for all concerned—they were never able to come even close to establishing this fact.

Because there was little time between the examination and the date the members of Congress had to make their decisions, the Commission's problem was gigantic. No government agency likes to admit error. It is particularly distressing when the error directly involves a member of Congress. Whenever it has happened in the designation examination, the Commission has found that the only solution lies in being candid. In this case, the Commission assembled several of its more able and articulate staff members, briefed them, and sent them to the Hill to explain the facts and offer the only remedy the Commission could suggest—retesting. Naturally, this was embarrassing to all concerned.

The Commission wrestled with a similarly troublesome problem once when a clerk with an unusually sharp eye noticed that several young men who had taken the examination in Minneapolis had made spectacularly high scores on the algebra portion of the test. It would have been extraordinary for *one* to make such a high score; it was phenomenal for several to make almost identically high scores. Her curiosity thus aroused, she made a further check and found that the young men all attended the same prep school. She alerted her supervisor, who passed the word on up. The problem was complicated by the fact that the young men were sponsored by seven different members of Congress. If it had been a regular civil service examination, an investigation would have been conducted, the involved persons interrogated, those judged guilty rated ineligible and barred from future examinations for a specified period. These participants were not clients of the Commission, however, but of the members of Congress.

The Commission decided the first thing to do was to find out how the simultaneously high scores could have occurred. One staff member reasoned that the most likely possibility was that one of the young men was a mathematical whiz and had helped the others. But how? He next supposed that the examiner who had administered the test had perhaps been too trusting. A call to the Commission's regional director brought verification that the examiner had left the room for approximately twenty minutes while the test was in progress, a direct violation of the instructions. The only thing the Commission could do was visit the several members of Congress, explain what had happened, and leave the appropriate action to their decision. They were generally understanding and quickly agreed that they must retest the group. They could probably tell quickly from the results whether cheating had occurred the first time. (One congressman stipulated that the examiner be warned that he would be fired if he committed such an indiscretion again. The Commission's staff members felt that firing was too mild a penalty but could find no legal punishment more severe.)

Another episode showed the hazards of relying on statistical probabilities when Congress is involved. Loud cries followed one designation examination in Los Angeles at which there were not enough test papers for all the candidates. Through years of experience, those who handle the stocking and shipping of test booklets to examination points had learned they could rely on a certain percentage of the candidates not appearing for an examination. Consequently, less examination papers were shipped to that location than the number of competitors scheduled to take the test. But, on this occasion, past experience and precedent were upset when all scheduled competitors showed up at examination time.

Even though the Commission tried to explain exactly what had happened, the more it explained, the more difficult it was to get the explanation accepted. The congressional offices involved made their position clear. They felt that, when they scheduled someone to take an examination, they expected him to take it, not to be prevented because an efficiency expert had calculated that he would not show up. The Commission made special arrangements to test those who had been excluded and took steps to see that in future designation examinations no calculated risk would be taken on the number of test booklets required.

THE PENDULUM

The Commission's relations with Congress will probably always mirror the balance, however delicate, within the federal government. If the general relations between Congress and the executive branch are relatively tranquil, it is likely that relations between Congress and the Commission will be, too. If, however, a strong chief executive becomes locked in battle with Congress, then the Commission is in a delicate position. If the Commission is considered a member of the President's official family, Congress may show that it expects more than the Commission can deliver; if it is not, it will have its hopes frustrated at both ends of Pennsylvania Avenue.

X

Readiness for Tomorrow

Under new Presidential administrations, personalities in the government change but the problems of personnel management remain essentially the same. Examination of some of the major issues faced during the closing days of the Johnson Administration should shed light on the problems and future course of action of the Nixon Administration.

THE VOICES OF DISSENT

The tendency of people everywhere increasingly to voice dissent has invaded the previously quiet domain of the career Civil Service. In the spring of 1968, a small group of federal career employees gave public voice to their disagreement with the Administration's Vietnam War policy. To experienced career employees and political executives alike, it was an audacious action, and it immediately directed attention to the rights of employees to express themselves on publicly controversial issues. To the old-timers, the issue was not debatable. No such right existed. If a person wished to challenge his employer publicly, he could do so, of course, but it was his obligation to resign first. But the problem was not that simple; it involved the question of whether dissent within the government should be stifled. Chairman Macy took note of the issue in a speech before the District of Columbia chapter of the Federal Bar Association in Washington on May 22, 1968. His speech, entitled "A Citizen's Rights, an Employee's Responsibilities," tells something of the problem and the Commission reaction:

> Again we come to the need for balance. The federal employee is a full citizen and entitled to express his views—publicly if this is his choice; however, he cannot proceed blindly down this path in perfect immunity. He is responsible for his actions, like any citizen. He does indeed have special obligations connected with his own role in his agency's programs, when these come into question. And he must keep his private activities strictly apart from his use of official time or government property. Last, but not least, he needs to be aware of any special regulations which may bear on his participation. . . .

> At the same time I think we need to deal with the implications of dissent in constructive ways. Are our institutions and processes so cut-and-dried and lusterless that the innovative Federal employee feels he needs to go outside the established framework in order to find expression for creative ideas? Does the environment we create have a stifling effect on the activists and innovators who are now working in government? How can this idealism and sense of urgency evidenced by the dissenters be channeled into the government's agenda of critical actions?

> I would hope that every manager would think about these questions and shape his own constructive answers. The questions need to be answered by all of us as perhaps the most important aspect of our reaction to dissent. In this time of change we have seen many men march to different drummers and tattoos than in the past. And the Federal work force cannot be deaf to the tunes of our times, because it is representative of our whole population and carries the future hope and aspirations of that population.

THE SURGE OF UNION ACTIVITY

"There is no right to strike against the public safety by anybody, anywhere, any time," Calvin Coolidge, Governor of

Massachusetts wrote to Samuel Gompers, President of the American Federation of Labor, on September 14, 1919. Until recently, this statement established a basic tenet of employee-management relations for public jurisdictions throughout the country. It is against the law for federal employees to engage in strikes against the government. Each new employee signs an affidavit that he will not strike. Although many state and local jurisdictions have prohibitions against strikes by their employees, strikes have occurred, and the governing body has apparently been powerless to enforce its own laws. The most widely publicized strikes have been those of municipal workers in New York City.

Although there have been no strikes of major consequence by federal workers, there is ample evidence of restlessness. Some federal unions have dropped from their by-laws a prohibition against strikes, indicating a more militant attitude. The law prohibiting strikes by federal employees still stands, but the question of whether it would be enforceable against a massive movement remains unanswered. Although a test could come at any time, there is no indication that any union expects to challenge the law or even has the capacity to organize and carry out a major strike. The first moves are likely to be wildcat strikes or activities by locals not having the sanction of their national organization.

A dramatic example of the kinds of problems that may be encountered is the action of a local of the National Association of Government Employees in a New York City Weather Bureau office. On March 1, 1968, members of the union staged a demonstration outside an NBC-TV studio in Manhattan during an appearance by Dr. Robert M. White, administrator of the Environmental Science Services Administration, of which the Weather Bureau is a part. The employees carried placards criticizing personnel practices in the Weather Bureau. The Bureau responded by withdrawing recognition of the local and canceling its dues-withholding agreement for violation of the prohibition against picketing contained in the code of fair labor practices enunciated by President Kennedy in a Presidential memorandum issued on May 21, 1963. The union took the case to court, and the matter had not been finally resolved as this was being written. It was being carefully watched, however, by union and management leaders. Experienced observers of the federal employment picture agree that union-management relations will present one of the most difficult problems of the next few years.

In November, 1967, according to Commission statistics, more than 1.2 million employees were under exclusive-recognition agreements between unions and management. Exclusive recognition gives a union the right to represent all employees of a specified unit. To obtain exclusive recognition in a unit, a union must be selected by a majority of the employees to represent them after first meeting the requirements for formal recognition specified in Executive Order 10988, issued by President Kennedy in 1962. The spectacular growth of the unions in recent years was made possible by two things: first was that order, which for the first time gave official recognition to the role of unions in government; second, and perhaps more influential, was the procedure whereby the government could collect union dues by withholding the amount from the paychecks of those employees who so desired. The latest available figures (1967) showed that more than $23 million in dues had been collected in that manner in one year. It is estimated that the total of dues going into union coffers, including those paid directly by employees, would approximate $25 million.

Unions had grown more than numerically, however. They had grown more militant. Their economic muscle makes them an obvious force to be reckoned with. Beginning in the 89th Congress and continuing into the 90th, their lobbying activities were causing concern both on Capitol Hill and in the executive branch. The postal unions were particularly aggressive in their pressure for special pay legislation in the first session of the 90th Congress. There was also considerable concern over the capacity and apparent desire of some unions to engage in political activity, particularly congressional elections.

Whether the militant actions of the public-employee unions in state and local jurisdictions will find widespread acceptance in the federal service is, of course, conjectural. However, as the unions grow numerically and financially, their power is bound to find an outlet. Their financial resources enable them to have highly paid staffs. If the staffs are to continue to be supported by the dues of the members, unions must do something for the members. Doing something will mean getting them something they do not presently have—either such pocketbook items as more pay or shorter hours or greater voice in the policies that affect them. The capacity of the unions to pressure Congress has already been demonstrated. The number of unions and professional associations ready to testify on federal-employee legislation has already required the Commission to increase its contacts with both union and congressional representatives.

With the expanded activity of the unions have come questions concerning the need for more public controls than presently exist to make certain that both the public interest and the interests of the unions' members are protected. The problems are complex and fundamental. Much more than the role of the Civil Service Commission is involved. At issue is the fundamental question of how willing the taxpayers are to have the Congress and the Chief Executive establish ground rules under which their civil servants work and how much they are willing to leave to negotiation with the employees themselves.

In September, 1967, President Johnson appointed a committee under the chairmanship of the Secretary of Labor to review the employee-management relations program and to report its findings and recommendations. The committee did not complete its work prior to the conclusion of the Johnson

Administration, so it remains the task of the Nixon Administration to review the problem. But controversy can be expected to continue, for there are significant differences of opinion about the status unions should enjoy and the type of regulation to which they should be subjected. Some believe that there should be a separate organization for the administration of labor relations in the federal service. Sponsors of the idea have suggested something on the order of a little National Labor Relations Board. Even if this should occur, the Commission will still be considerably involved with the unions, for much of the policy that union demands will be targeted toward is presided over by the Commission.

The Commission is in a much better position to deal with unions today than it was a few years ago. Before 1962, there was no sharp demarcation between unions and management, as there is in private industry. Many supervisors and high-ranking employees were union members. Nowhere was this more evident than in the Commission itself, where it had been customary for even the regional directors to belong to the union. It is said that in earlier days union kingmakers were among the Commission's top staff. This has changed, however. The Commission now has an office that specializes in labor relations, reporting directly to the Chairman. It maintains a neutral position, trying to ensure that the provisions of President Kennedy's executive order are strictly followed by both management and labor. The Commission is equipped to provide central direction to labor relations, even on an expanded basis, should it be called upon to do so.

New Areas of Cooperation

The recent expansion of programs involving federal grants to state and local government units has brought concern about the quality of personnel administration at those levels of government. In the 90th Congress, the Senate passed a bill, sponsored by Senator Edmund S. Muskie, that would place the

Commission in direct contact with local governmental units and enlarge the scope of the Commission's activities in spectacular fashion. Although the bill did not come up for a vote in the House before Congress adjourned, it had wide support, and its chance of passage in the next Congress appears to be good. Entitled the Inter-Governmental Personnel Act of 1967, it would authorize the Commission to grant funds to state and local governments to strengthen their personnel administrations. The Commission would be authorized to train employees of those jurisdictions and perform technical services for them on a fee basis. In addition, the law would permit employees to move, within carefully defined limits, between state and local jurisdictions and the federal competitive civil service. Some public administration students have long felt that it would serve the public interest if employees of different merit systems could transfer freely between them. This would presumably provide a basis for making badly needed specialists immediately available to all levels of government as well as offer an excellent opportunity for arranging career-development programs that would give an employee much broader experience than he can have when his career is confined to one jurisdiction. If the legislation passes, the Commission would set the standards for grants and would have responsibility for seeing that they are met. The over-all effect would be to establish the central personnel agency of the federal government as the leader to whom all public personnel jurisdictions might look for help.

In a separate but related action, the 90th Congress enacted a law known as the Inter-Governmental Cooperation Act of 1968. One of its important features is that it permits federal agencies to perform technical and special services for state and local units of government on a fee basis. The Act offers great promise for a completely new era of federal-state relations. Even with respect to the Commission's functions alone, its impact could be significant, as the following illustrations suggest.

For many years, the Commission has given a nationwide examination targeted toward college graduation classes. Many state jurisdictions have similar programs. Knowledgeable personnel officials of both local and federal governments have felt that great efficiency could be provided if there were only one examination for entry into the public service, whatever the level of government. Under the new law, one test would be possible, and each participating agency would reimburse the Commission for its share of the cost. The adoption of such a program will eliminate many problems, not the least of which is that of the student who now must go through the ordeal of qualifying in separate examinations for each jurisdiction for which he wishes to be considered.

Another area that could be greatly affected by this law is the training activity of the Commission. It would be relatively simple for the Commission to open its courses to employees of other jurisdictions for a fee. However, this action could enlarge the demand so that the training staff and facilities would have to be expanded.

As mentioned earlier in this chapter, the problems of unionism, along with other personnel management problems, have intensified in state and local jurisdictions. It is logical that some of these jurisdictions might look to the central personnel agency of the federal government for leadership and assistance, but the Commission has not been staffed to give more than token assistance to another jurisdiction, and, until 1968, it had been without authority. Presumably, under the Inter-Governmental Cooperation Act, the Commission could provide the assistance desired and be reimbursed for it.

Although these three have been mentioned as areas of possible action, under the law there is practically no activity of the Commission that might not be called upon to provide assistance. A primary problem of the Commission is that the law did not appropriate funds; it merely authorized the Commission to render services and receive reimbursement as they are performed. Consequently, the Commission will have to solve the problem of how to finance the staff needed to do the jobs for which it will ultimately receive payment. The Commission must also be certain that it does not take on so much business that it will divert its attention from its primary mission of serving as the central personnel agency for the federal service.

THE CHANGING FEDERAL WORKFORCE

In recent years, the composition of the federal workforce has undergone a steady and significant change, brought on primarily by two factors: the rapid advance of automatic data-processing and the expanding demands for governmental services ranging from the solution of urban problems to the conquest of outer space. Professional, technical, and administrative personnel now comprise more than 50 per cent of the white-collar force. Less than 40 per cent are in clerical positions. During the ten-year period ending in June, 1966, white-collar employment increased by 4.7 per cent, while blue-collar employment decreased by 7.3 per cent.

The impact of the computer may be seen in the Commission's own organization. In the spring of 1968, the Commission announced the establishment of the Bureau of Manpower Information Systems. Although the Commission had for some years been using computers for much work formerly done by hand—such as the scheduling and scoring of written examinations—it began to notice how vast was the field of paper-work and record-keeping throughout the service. A staggering but uniform record-keeping system has been in effect in the federal government for some years. Each agency is required to maintain a folder on each employee, containing prescribed types of information on standard forms. If the employee transfers from one agency to another, the file is transferred with him. When he leaves the service, it goes to the Federal Records Center, operated by the General Service Administration in Saint Louis, Missouri. Every official transaction concerning each employee is recorded uniformly.

It has been reasoned that, if the techniques applied by the airlines to reservations and scheduling were applied to the personnel record-keeping processes, huge savings would result both by doing the actual recording much faster and cheaper and by producing an abundance of information not currently available. But automating the system would require money, which would be forthcoming only if the idea had the enthusiastic support of both the Bureau of the Budget and Congress. The keepers of the purse strings must be shown that the estimated savings will, in fact, accrue. Also, federal managers must be convinced that service to the agencies will not be impaired and individual prerogatives will not be infringed.

If such a revolutionary change were to take place, the relationships between the agency personnel offices and the Commission would also change. The Commission would be able to provide fast and efficient service to the agency manager. This is already true in certain activities such as supplying lists of names from examinations, but it would be multiplied many times if the Commission assumed responsibility for maintaining the records kept and processing the transactions undertaken by an agency for its own employees.

Whether or not the Commission takes on the task of establishing a completely modern, uniform system of personnel record-processing and -keeping, it will continue to face major problems in adjusting qualification standards and recruiting programs to the rapid changes taking place across the country and the corollary demands for services from the government.

A still unresolved question that will undoubtedly emerge again is the extent to which work must be performed by employees on the federal payroll, as opposed to being contracted out to private businesses. The Commission's position is generally supported by the unions, but it is actively opposed by business interests. It prohibits contracting for secretaries and permits only certain specified activities to be performed outside the federal government. It is likely that Congress will attempt to define the proper line of demarcation more precisely, but drawing the line will be difficult, and the Commission is certain to play a key role in the dialogue. Whether the Commission will enjoy its role will depend partially on the attitude of the President, for full adherence to the legal opinion of the Commission could add several hundred thousand people to the federal payroll. The decision entails political medicine hard for an elected official to swallow.

THE MACY IMPRINT

The future of the Commission will depend on its institutional maturity and prestige and the capabilities of its staff. The present institution bears the strong imprint of John W. Macy, Jr., who served as its Chairman for eight years—more than twice as long as any other person since the position was established during the Truman Administration. In addition, as executive director, he was responsible for the operations of the staff during five years of the Eisenhower Administration. The current key staff members were practically all selected for their jobs by him or with his concurrence. Most of the junior executives have been recruited and trained under programs that have had to meet his approval.

Key staff members have been trained to think in broad terms. They have been carefully briefed on all of the problems of the President. They possess more information about programs and goals of the Chief Executive than their predecessors did. This was made possible by Macy's closeness to the President and his unrelenting effort to communicate to the staff both information and the need for related Commission action.

When a new program was to be launched, the staff was expected to pick up the ball and make certain a new executive was not waiting for help. If sometimes the Commission man was hanging around the door trying to get the action started before the new manager was ready, that was all to the good. The attitude that the Commission should wait to be contacted by an agency when the agency was ready to do business became obsolete. Macy asked for reports on the status of the agencies' staffing efforts, and the only way Commission employees could respond was by ringing agency doorbells and finding out.

When the Vietnam War began to escalate, Macy requested figures on recruiting for civilian jobs in the Army, Navy, and Air Force. Contacts between key staff members of the agencies and the Commission brought the response that everything was proceeding well. Not satisfied, Macy wanted the actual manpower figures—present strength, anticipated build-up by job categories, timetable, and so on. The figures simply were not available. The Defense Department agencies did not have them. Macy's continued insistence upon facts required both the Commission and the Department of Defense to make a manpower analysis and plan that probably prevented serious difficulties as the build-up developed.

Ordinarily, this would have been considered the responsibility of the Secretary of Defense, but Macy's concept of the central personnel agency's job was that the agency anticipates problems and heads them off. Further, of course, there was the very practical consideration that, if the Defense Department agencies suddenly got into a recruiting crisis, the Commission's problems would be multiplied many times.

CONTINUITY OF LEADERSHIP

In addition to Macy's strong imprint on the present Commission, a continuity of tenure of the other commissioners and top staff has provided a stable, if not unique, relationship at the executive level.

Commissioner Ludwig J. Andolsek, Vice-Chairman under Macy, and, like Macy, a Democrat, was first appointed on

April 30, 1963, and he was reappointed in 1969 by President Nixon to another six-year term. He had served in the executive and legislative branches most of his working life, and he brought to his job wide knowledge and understanding of the functions and problems of both. A natural champion of the underdog, he has provided a link between the institution and individuals with problems and has endeavored to see that policy considerations reflect an understanding of such problems.

Robert E. Hampton, the Republican member, who was named Chairman to succeed Macy soon after Nixon took office, had been reappointed for a second six-year term in 1967, so the team of commissioners in office as the Johnson Administration ended had been together for more than five years. Hampton, like both Macy and Andolsek, has had wide experience in government. He served on the White House staff during the latter part of the Eisenhower Administration, and he brought to the Commission a constructive, conservative point of view and an intense interest in Commission problems and federal personnel management in general.

To fill the third Commissioner's position, James E. Johnson, a Republican of California, was appointed. Johnson, the first Negro ever to be appointed to the Commission, is highly regarded and considered well qualified although new to the federal civil service.

In addition to the fact that two of the three commissioners have been together for a period of time sufficient to provide a consistent approach to problems, there has been continuity in the top-level staff. Nicholas J. Oganovic, executive director since 1965, is a career employee who literally grew up in the Commission and has held a variety of jobs both in and out of Washington, including several years of service as deputy executive director, which gave him excellent preparation for his present job. Oganovic, whose readiness to disturb the *status quo* could be exceeded only by Macy's, made a great impact upon the Commission's operations. Although he is also responsible for direction of the staff, his greatest asset perhaps has been the contribution he has made to the full range of Commission programs through his steady flow of innovative ideas and his determination to solve problems, however difficult.

Before 1965, Warren B. Irons had served as executive director from the time Macy left that job in 1958. Irons, an extremely able executive, had come to the Commission years before and rescued the retirement program when it was in jeopardy. Widely known for his blunt, lay-it-on-the-line, practical approach, he was highly respected on Capitol Hill and handled many of the Commission's most difficult congressional problems. He enjoyed such prestige that his role was a unique one for an employee of the career service.

The nature of the Commission's business is such that its staff is trained in objectivity and the art of steering between the parties to avoid the pitfalls of partisanship. Its basic mission is to facilitate good government by establishing the conditions in which a well-qualified and highly motivated federal workforce can give the taxpayers the programs and services they desire and upon which the future of our society rests. This is a task of tremendous scope and one that will never be carried out to the complete satisfaction of the people charged with the responsibility of accomplishing it.

How the Chief Executive chooses to use the Commission will have great bearing on its activities and influence. It should be remembered that the Commission was given major functions during the Kennedy and Johnson administrations that can be discontinued or assigned elsewhere by executive action. But, because of the staff's closeness to political leadership in recent years and its experience in Republican and Democratic administrations, the Commission has acquired a degree of flexibility and pragmatism that should make it very useful to a new Administration, whatever problem it confronts.

Even so, there was some apprehension on the part of the staff and concerned observers as President Nixon took office. In any federal agency, the problems of transition from one

Administration to another are always difficult, if for no other reason than that it takes a while for the new political appointees and the career staff to get acquainted with each other. Sometimes a period of inaction or near chaos prevails. When President Nixon unprecedentedly designated incumbent Republican Commissioner Robert E. Hampton as Chairman, the Commission's transfer from Democratic to Republican control was greatly simplified. Not since the position had been created had the minority member been so recognized by his party as it took office.

The appointment was instantly popular. Although it was generally applauded by the press, career personnel, and congressional leaders, even greater enthusiasm came from among the Commission's staff, for Hampton had maintained the closest working relationships with them. Although they recognized that his political philosophy might differ greatly from that of his predecessor and could result in changes in programs to which they had devoted much time and energy, their high regard for him made the potential adjustments much easier to contemplate. Therefore, the Commission was in position to be off and running as the new Administration started. Its future will probably depend on what is asked of it.

Appendix A

Career Opportunities
in Personnel Management

The expression that is perhaps most commonly heard in employment offices is: "I would like to go into personnel work because I like people and want to work with them." Some jobs in personnel management involve much contact with the employees of an organization, but others are largely behind the scenes, with little if any contact with employees. One job, for example, involves studying the duties performed by an individual or group of individuals and determining their qualification requirements; another job involves determining rates of pay. Still another job involves devising techniques that measure the ability of a person to perform a given set of duties. Another job entails interviewing for employment and recommending placement of individuals. Solving employee-relations problems is another specialization. Recently, the need for persons skilled in labor-relations techniques has become of increasing importance.

For many years, the Civil Service Commission has conducted annually a recruiting program designed to bring to its staff young people who have the background, motivation, and mobility to accept the challenges of its wide variety of assignments. For the young person who desires a career in personnel management, growth opportunities are excellent because they are government-wide. Almost every federal agency employs specialists in personnel management; how many depends on the size of the agency. It is important to remember that all personnel offices have direct and frequent contact with the Commission, because it is vitally interested in the training and development of those who work in the field and it encourages mobility between agencies. Consequently, the young person does not need fear that he will get into a blind alley by having to remain in one agency, if he has

213

the ability and willingness to work hard enough to advance. The field is large enough to allow a great deal of movement and vacancies occur frequently.

The Commission operates a two-year internship program for selected new employees of the various agencies, starting a class of approximately 100 each year. Employees hired by the agencies are assigned to a program designed and coordinated by the Commission. The carefully structured training plan involves various work assignments at the Commission and in other agencies, and it is supplemented by seminars and lectures. At the conclusion of the two-year training period, the employee joins the regular staff of the agency that initially hired him. A new program is started each year so that people are in training at all times. Approximately half of the trainees are in Washington offices; the other half are scattered throughout the field service.

The starting levels for professional personnel work are grades GS-5 and GS-7 on the federal job-classification scale. The pay for these levels is adjusted whenever the federal pay scale as a whole is adjusted. In 1969, the annual salary was $6,176 for GS-5, $7,639 for GS-7. The qualified person may be promoted to jobs at all higher levels. The director of personnel of a large department is generally classified GS-17.

The qualification requirements for most of the jobs do not specify any amount or kind of education, but the odds for success greatly favor persons who have attended college. College graduates with superior academic records may qualify at GS-7, while those with average grades qualify at GS-5. Persons who have attended graduate school may enter at higher levels, depending on the amount and type of graduate study. Individuals desiring to enter public personnel administration are well advised to take courses in business and public administration, psychology, and political science, For the undergraduate, the broadest possible general education is considered best.

Anyone wishing information about how to begin a career in personnel management in the offices of the government may obtain literature or answers to specific questions by writing or visiting a Civil Service Commission office. (See Appendix B for the location of regional offices.)

Appendix B

U.S. Civil Service Regions

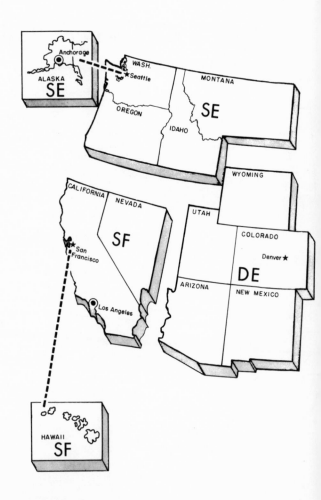

REGIONAL AREA KEY

Atlanta - AT	New York - NY
Boston - BN	Philadelphia - PH
Chicago - CH	Seattle - SE
Dallas - DA	San Francisco - SF
Denver - DE	St. Louis - SL

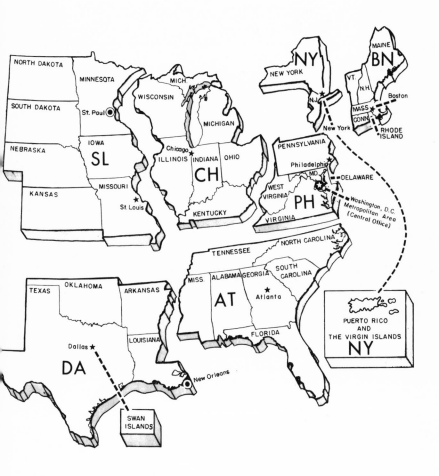

★ REGIONAL HEADQUARTERS
◉ BRANCH OFFICES
✪ CENTRAL OFFICE

Appendix C

Civil Service Laws

The original Civil Service Act, as established by the Pendleton Act of 1883, passed by the 47th Congress, is reprinted here in its entirety. Although it has undergone some modifications, the major part of the original Act remains intact and forms the foundation upon which the U.S. civil service is built. The Act is now incorporated in Title 5 of the United States Code. Other important laws administered either in whole or in part by the Civil Service Commission and also to be found in Title 5 are:

> Annual and Sick Leave Act (1951)
> Civil Service Retirement Act (1956)
> Classification Act (1949)
> Federal Employees Group Life Insurance Act (1954)
> Federal Employees Health Benefits Act (1959)
> Government Employees Incentive Awards Act (1954)
> Government Employees Training Act (1958)
> Hatch Political Activities Act (1939, 1940)
> Lloyd–LaFollette Act (1912)
> Ramspeck Act (1940)
> Veteran's Preference Act (1944)

THE CIVIL SERVICE ACT

AN ACT To regulate and improve the civil service of the United States.

Be it enacted by the Senate and House of Representatives of the United States of America in Congress assembled, That the President is authorized to appoint, by and with the advice and consent of the Senate, three persons, not more than two of whom shall be adherents of the same party, as Civil Service Commissioners, and said three commissioners shall constitute

218

the United States Civil Service Commission. Said commissioners shall hold no other official place under the United States.

The President may remove any commissioner; and any vacancy in the position of commissioner shall be so filled by the President, by and with the advice and consent of the Senate, as to conform to said conditions for the first selection of commissioners.

The commissioners shall each receive a salary of three thousand five hundred dollars a year. And each of said commissioners shall be paid his necessary traveling expenses incurred in the discharge of his duty as a commissioner.

SEC. 2. That it shall be the duty of said commissioners:

FIRST. To aid the President, as he may request, in preparing suitable rules for carrying this act into effect, and when said rules shall have been promulgated it shall be the duty of all officers of the United States in the departments and offices to which any such rules may relate to aid, in all proper ways, in carrying said rules, and any modifications thereof, into effect.

SECOND. And, among other things, said rules shall provide and declare, as nearly as the conditions of good administration will warrant, as follows:

First, for open, competitive examinations for testing the fitness of applicants for the public service now classified or to be classified hereunder. Such examinations shall be practical in their character, and so far as may be shall relate to those matters which will fairly test the relative capacity and fitness of the persons examined to discharge the duties of the service into which they seek to be appointed.

Second, that all the offices, places, and employments so arranged or to be arranged in classes shall be filled by selections according to grade from among those graded highest as the results of such competitive examinations.

Third, appointments to the public service aforesaid in the departments at Washington shall be apportioned among the several States and Territories and the District of Columbia upon the basis of population as ascertained at the last preceding census. Every application for an examination shall contain, among other things, a statement, under oath, setting forth his or her actual bona fide residence at the time of making the application, as well as how long he or she has been a resident of such place.

Fourth, that there shall be a period of probation before any absolute appointment or employment aforesaid.

Fifth, that no person in the public service is for that reason under any obligations to contribute to any political fund, or to render any political service, and that he will not be removed or otherwise prejudiced for refusing to do so.

Sixth, that no person in said service has any right to use his official authority or influence to coerce the political action of any person or body.

Seventh, there shall be non-competitive examinations in all proper cases before the commission, when competent persons do not compete, after notice has been given of the existence of the vacancy, under such rules as may be prescribed by the commissioners as to the manner of giving notice.

Eighth, that notice shall be given in writing by the appointing power to said commission of the persons selected for appointment or employment from among those who have been examined, of the place of residence of such persons, of the rejection of any such persons after probation, of transfers, resignations, and removals, and of the date thereof, and a record of the same shall be kept by said commission.

And any necessary exceptions from said eight fundamental provisions of the rules shall be set forth in connection with such rules, and the reasons therefor shall be stated in the annual reports of the commission.

THIRD. Said commission shall, subject to the rules that may be made by the President, make regulations for, and have control of, such examinations, and, through its members or the examiners, it shall supervise and preserve the records of the same; and said commission shall keep minutes of its own proceedings.

FOURTH. Said commission may make investigations concerning the facts, and may report upon all matters touching the enforcement and effects of said rules and regulations, and concerning the action of any examiner or board of examiners hereinafter provided for, and its own subordinates, and those in the public service, in respect to the execution of this act.

FIFTH. Said commission shall make an annual report to the President for transmission to Congress, showing its own action, the rules and regulations and the exceptions thereto in force, the practical effects thereof, and any suggestions it may approve for the more effectual accomplishment of the purposes of this act.

SEC. 3. That said commission is authorized to employ a chief examiner, a part of whose duty it shall be, under its direction, to act with the examining boards, so far as practicable, whether at Washington or elsewhere, and to secure accuracy, uniformity, and justice in all their proceedings, which shall be at all times open to him. The chief examiner shall be entitled to receive a salary at the rate of three thousand dollars a year, and he shall be paid his necessary traveling expenses incurred in the discharge of his duty. The commission shall have a secretary, to be appointed by the President, who shall receive a salary of one thousand six hundred dollars per annum. It may, when necessary, employ a stenographer, and a messenger, who shall be paid, when employed, the former at the rate of one thousand six hundred dollars a year, and the latter at the rate of six hundred dollars a year. The commission shall, at Washington, and in one or more places in each State and Territory where examinations are to take place, designate and select a suitable number of persons, not less than three, in the official service of the United States, residing in said State or Territory, after consulting the head of the department or office in which such persons serve, to be members of boards of examiners, and may at any time substitute any other person in said service living in such State or Territory in the place of any one so selected. Such boards of examiners shall be so located as to make it reasonably convenient and inexpensive for applicants to attend before them; and where there are persons to be examined in any State or Territory, examinations shall be held therein at least twice in each year. It shall be the duty of the collector, postmaster, and other officers of the United States, at any place outside of the District of Columbia where examinations are directed by the President or by said board to be held, to allow the reasonable use of the public buildings for holding such examinations, and in all proper ways to facilitate the same.

Sec. 4. That it shall be the duty of the Secretary of the Interior to cause suitable and convenient rooms and accommodations to be assigned or provided, and to be furnished, heated, and lighted, at the city of Washington, for carrying on the work of said commission and said examinations, and to cause the necessary stationery and other articles to be supplied, and the necessary printing to be done for said commission.

Sec. 5. That any said commissioner, examiner, copyist, or messenger, or any person in the public service who shall willfully and corruptly, by himself or in co-operation with one or more other persons, defeat, deceive, or obstruct any person in respect of his or her right of examination according to any such rules or regulations, or who shall willfully, corruptly, and falsely mark, grade, estimate, or report upon the examination of proper standing of any person examined hereunder, or aid in so doing, or who shall willfully and corruptly make any false representations concerning the same or concerning the person examined, or who shall willfully and corruptly furnish to any person any special or secret information for the purpose of either improving or injuring the prospects or chances of any person so examined, or to be examined, being appointed, employed, or promoted, shall for each such offense be deemed guilty of a misdemeanor, and upon conviction thereof, shall be punished by a fine of not less than one hundred dollars, nor more than one thousand dollars, or by imprisonment not less than ten days, nor more than one year, or by both such fine and imprisonment.

Sec. 6. That within sixty days after the passage of this act it shall be the duty of the Secretary of the Treasury, in as near conformity as may be to the classification of certain clerks now existing under the one hundred and sixty-third section of the Revised Statutes, to arrange in classes the several clerks and persons employed by the collector, naval officer, surveyor, and appraisers, or either of them, or being in the public service, at their respective offices in each customs district where the whole number of said clerks and persons shall be all together as many as fifty. And thereafter, from time to time, on the direction of the President, said Secretary shall make the like classification or arrangement of clerks and persons so employed, in connection with any said office or offices, in any other customs district. And, upon like request, and for the purposes of this act, said Secretary shall arrange in one or more of said classes, or of existing classes, any other clerks, agents, or persons employed under his department in any said district not now classified; and every such arrangement and classification upon being made shall be reported to the President.

SECOND. Within said sixty days it shall be the duty of the Postmaster-General, in general conformity to said one hundred and sixty-third section, to separately arrange in classes the several clerks and persons employed, or in the public service, at each post-office, or under any postmaster of the United States, where the whole number of said clerks and persons shall together amount to as many as fifty. And thereafter, from time to time, on the direction of the President, it shall be the duty of the Postmaster-General to arrange in like classes the clerks and persons so employed in the postal service in connection with any other post-office; and every such arrangement and classification upon being made shall be reported to the President.

THIRD. That from time to time said Secretary, the Postmaster-General and each of the heads of departments mentioned in the one hundred and fifty-eighth section of the Revised Statutes, and each head of an office, shall, on the direction of the President, and for facilitating the execution of this act, respectively revise any then existing classification or arrangement of those in their respective departments and offices, and shall, for the purposes of the examination herein provided for, include in one or more of such classes, so far as practicable, subordinate places, clerks, and officers in the public service pertaining to their respective departments not before classified for examination.

SEC. 7. That after the expiration of six months from the passage of this act no officer or clerk shall be appointed, and no person shall be employed to enter or be promoted in either of the said classes now existing, or that may be arranged hereunder pursuant to said rules, until he has passed an examination, or is shown to be specially exempted from such examination in conformity herewith. But nothing herein contained shall be construed to take from those honorably discharged from the military or naval service any preference conferred by the seventeen hundred and fifty-fourth section of the Revised Statutes, nor to take from the President any authority not inconsistent with this act conferred by the seventeen hundred and fifty-third section of said statutes; nor shall any officer not in the executive branch of the government, or any person merely employed as a laborer or workman, be required to be classified hereunder; nor, unless by direction of the Senate, shall any person who has been nominated for confirmation by the Senate be required to be classified or to pass an examination.

SEC. 8. That no person habitually using intoxicating beverages to excess shall be appointed to, or retained in, any office, appointment, or employment to which the provisions of this act are applicable.

SEC. 9. That whenever there are already two or more members of a family in the public service in the grades covered by this act, no other member of such family shall be eligible to appointment to any of said grades.

SEC. 10. That no recommendation of any person who shall apply for office or place under the provisions of this act which may be given by any Senator or member of the House of Representatives, except as to the character or residence of the applicant, shall be received or considered by any person concerned in making any examination or appointment under this act.

SEC. 11. That no Senator, or Representative, or Territorial Delegate of the Congress, or Senator, Representative, or Delegate elect, or any officer or employee of either of said houses, and no executive, judicial, military, or naval officer of the United States, and no clerk or employee of any department, branch or bureau of the executive, judicial, or military or naval service of the United States, shall, directly or indirectly, solicit or receive, or be in any manner concerned in soliciting or receiving, any assessment, subscription, or contribution for any political purpose whatever, from any officer, clerk, or employee of the United States, or any department, branch, or bureau thereof, or from any person receiving any salary or compensation from moneys derived from the Treasury of the United States.

SEC. 12.   That no person shall, in any room or building occupied in the discharge of official duties by any officer or employee of the United States mentioned in this act, or in any navyyard, fort, or arsenal, solicit in any manner whatever, or receive any contribution of money or any other thing of value for any political purpose whatever.

SEC. 13.   No officer or employee of the United States mentioned in this act shall discharge, or promote, or degrade, or in any manner change the official rank or compensation of any other officer or employee, or promise or threaten so to do, for giving or withholding or neglecting to make any contribution of money or other valuable thing for any political purpose.

SEC. 14.   That no officer, clerk, or other person in the service of the United States shall, directly or indirectly, give or hand over to any other officer, clerk, or person in the service of the United States, or to any Senator or Member of the House of Representatives, or Territorial Delegate, any money or other valuable thing on account of or to be applied to the promotion of any political object whatever.

SEC. 15.   That any person who shall be guilty of violating any provision of the four foregoing sections shall be deemed guilty of a misdemeanor, and shall, on conviction thereof, be punished by a fine not exceeding five thousand dollars, or by imprisonment for a term not exceeding three years, or by such fine and imprisonment both, in the discretion of the court.

Appendix D

Civil Service Commissioners

Name and Political Affiliation	State Appointed in	Date of Oath of Office	Date of Leaving Office[1]
Dorman B. Eaton (R)	N.Y.	Mar. 9, 1883	Apr. 17, 1886
John M. Gregory (R)	Ill.	Mar. 9, 1883	Nov. 9, 1885
Leroy D. Thoman (D)	Ohio	Mar. 9, 1883	Nov. 9, 1885
William L. Trenholm (D)	S.C.	Nov. 9, 1885	Apr. 17, 1886
Alfred P. Edgerton (D)	Ind.	Nov. 9, 1885	Feb. 9, 1889 (removed)
John H. Oberly (D)	Ill.	Apr. 17, 1886	Oct. 10, 1888
Charles Lyman (R)	Conn.	Apr. 17, 1886	May 24, 1895
Hugh S. Thompson (D)	S.C.	May 9, 1889	June 23, 1892
Theodore Roosevelt (R)	N.Y.	May 13, 1889	May 5, 1895
George D. Johnston (D)	La.	July 14, 1892	Nov. 28, 1893 (removed)
John R. Proctor (D)	Ky.	Dec. 2, 1893	Dec. 12, 1903 (died)
William G. Rice (D)	N.Y.	May 16, 1895	Jan. 19, 1898
John B. Harlow (R)	Mo.	May 25, 1895	Nov. 14, 1901
Mark S. Brewer (R)	Mich.	Jan. 19, 1898	Mar. 18, 1901 (died)
William A. Rodenberg (R)	Ill.	Mar. 25, 1901	Mar. 31, 1902
William D. Foulke (R)	Ind.	Nov. 15, 1901	Apr. 30, 1903
James R. Garfield (R)	Ohio	Apr. 24, 1902	Feb. 25, 1903
Alford W. Cooley (R)	N.Y.	June 18, 1903	Nov. 6, 1906
Henry F. Greene (R)	Minn.	June 20, 1903	Apr. 30, 1909
John C. Black (D)	Ill.	Jan. 16, 1904	June 10, 1913
John A. McIlhenny (D)	La.	Nov. 30, 1906	Feb. 28, 1919
James T. Williams, Jr. (R)	N.C.	May 5, 1909	May 25, 1909
William S. Washburn (R)	N.Y.	May 26, 1909	June 30, 1913
Charles M. Galloway (D)	S.C.	June 20, 1913	Sept. 7, 1919
Hermon W. Craven (R)	Wash.	July 3, 1913	Mar. 16, 1919
Martin A. Morrison (D)	Ind.	Mar. 13, 1919	July 14, 1921
George R. Wales (R)	Vt.	Mar. 17, 1919	Sept. 16, 1933 (died)

Helen H. Gardener (D)	D.C.	Apr. 13, 1920	July 26, 1925 (died)
John H. Bartlett (R)	N.H.	July 15, 1921	Mar. 12, 1922
William C. Deming (R)	Wyo.	Mar. 31, 1923	July 6, 1930
Jessie Dell (D)	Ga.	Sept. 18, 1925	May 11, 1933
Thomas E. Campbell (R)	Ariz.	July 7, 1930	May 11, 1933
Lucille F. McMillin (D)	Tenn.	May 12, 1933	Oct. 8, 1946
Harry B. Mitchell (D)	Mont.	May 12, 1933	Mar. 15, 1951
Leonard D. White (R)	Ill.	Mar. 26, 1934	June 15, 1937
Samuel H. Ordway, Jr. (R)	N.Y.	Sept. 15, 1937	May 31, 1939
Arthur S. Flemming (R)	D.C.	July 8, 1939	Aug. 30, 1948
Frances Perkins (D)	N.Y.	Oct. 9, 1946	Apr. 15, 1953
James M. Mitchell (R)	Ill.	Oct. 18, 1948	May 31, 1953
Robert Ramspeck (D)	Ga.	Mar. 16, 1951	Dec. 31, 1952
Philip Young (R)	N.Y.	Mar. 23, 1953	Feb. 28, 1957
George M. Moore (R)	Ky.	Apr. 14, 1953	Feb. 28, 1957
Frederick J. Lawton[2] (D)	D.C.	Apr. 27, 1953	Apr. 15, 1963 (retired)
Harris Ellsworth[3] (R)	Oreg.	Apr. 18, 1957	Feb. 28, 1959 (term expired)
Christopher H. Phillips[4]	Mass.	Apr. 18, 1957	Dec. 30, 1957
Bernard L. Flanagan (R)	Vt.	Jan. 2, 1958	July 25, 1958
Barbara B. Gunderson[5] (R)	S. Dak.	Sept. 12, 1958	Mar. 1, 1961 (term expired)
Roger W. Jones[6] (R)	Conn.	Mar. 9, 1959	Jan. 31, 1961
John W. Macy, Jr.[7] (D)	Conn.	Mar. 6, 1961	Jan. 19, 1969
Robert E. Hampton[8] (R)	Md.	July 25, 1961	
L. J. Andolsek[9] (D)	Minn.	Apr. 30, 1963	
James E. Johnson[10] (R)	Calif.	Feb. 24, 1969	

---

[1] By resignation, unless otherwise indicated.

[2] Term extended for 6 years beginning Mar. 1, 1957, under authority of Title II, Public Law 854 of July 31, 1956. Designated Vice-Chairman on March 22, 1961.

[3] Appointed for 2 years beginning Mar. 1, 1957, and designated Chairman, under authority of Title II, Public Law 854 of July 31, 1956.

[4] Appointed for 4 years beginning Mar. 1, 1957, and designated Vice-Chairman, under authority of Title II, Public Law 854, of July 31, 1956.

[5] Appointed to serve unexpired portion of term of Commissioner ending Feb. 28, 1961, and designated Vice-Chairman.

[6] Appointed for 6 years beginning Mar. 1, 1959, and designated Chairman.

[7] Appointed to serve unexpired term of Commissioner ending Mar. 1, 1965, and designated Chairman; reappointed for 6-year term ending Mar. 1, 1971, and designated Chairman.

[8] Designated Chairman January 20, 1969.

[9] Reappointed to new six-year term.

[10] Appointed to fill out term expiring March 1, 1971.

Bibliography

Much of the material for this book was drawn from the files and unpublished records of the U.S. Civil Service Commission and the Commission's annual reports, its monthly report on federal employment statistics, and the annual report of its Bureau of Retirement and Insurance. The Commission's library is an excellent source for anyone wishing to delve deeply into the Commission's history or into some aspect of public personnel administration. Its collection contains approximately 40,000 items on personnel subjects, 20,000 on related law and reference subjects, and 20,000 on social and political science. Although it does not release material for use outside Washington, it is open to all visitors.

COOKE, CHARLES. *Biography of an Ideal.* Washington, D.C.: U.S. Government Printing Office, 1959.

FELDMAN, HERMAN. *A Personnel Program for the Federal Civil Service.* (Report to the 71st Congress, House of Representatives, by the Director of the Personnel Classification Board.) Washington, D.C.: U.S. Government Printing Office, 1931.

HARRISON, EVELYN. "Talent Search for Womanpower," *AAUW Journal.* (March, 1965), pp. 99–101.

MACY, JOHN W., JR. "A Citizen's Rights, An Employees Responsibilities." (Address at the Tom Clark Award luncheon sponsored by the District of Columbia Chapter of the Federal Bar Association, May 22, 1968.) Washington, D.C.: U.S. Civil Service Commission.

OGANOVIC, NICHOLAS J. "Improving the Breed," *Personnel Administration.* (Jan.–Feb., 1966), pp. 6–8, 24.

REEVES, FLOYD W., and PAUL T. DAVID. *Personnel Administration in the Federal Service.* President's Committee on Administrative Management Study No. 1. Washington, D.C.: U.S. Government Printing Office, 1937.

ROOSEVELT, THEODORE. "No Political Influence Will Help You in the Least," *Letters of Theodore Roosevelt, Civil Service Commissioner 1890–1895*. Washington, D.C.: U.S. Government Printing Office, 1958.

U.S. BUREAU OF THE BUDGET. "Special Analysis F," *Budget of the United States Government for Fiscal Year 1969*. Washington, D.C.: U.S. Government Printing Office, 1969.

U.S. CIVIL SERVICE COMMISSION. *An Instrument for Progress*. Washington, D.C.: U.S. Civil Service Commission, 1964.

————. "Employment Under the Executive Assignment System," *The Federal Personnel Manual*. Washington, D.C.: U.S. Government Printing Office, 1967.

————. *The Federal Career Service at Your Service*. Washington, D.C.: U.S. Government Printing Office, 1967.

————. *Federal Incentive Awards Program, Fiscal Year 1967*. Washington, D.C.: U.S. Civil Service Commission, 1967.

————. *How People Are Recruited, Examined, and Appointed in the Competitive Civil Service*. (Report to the Subcommittee on Civil Service of the Post Office and Civil Service Committee of the House of Representatives.) Washington, D.C.: U.S. Government Printing Office, 1959.

————. *Improving Service to the Public: Summary No. 2*. Washington, D.C.: U.S. Civil Service Commission, 1967.

————. *The Role of the Civil Service in Federal Employment*. Pamphlet 52. Washington, D.C.: U.S. Government Printing Office, 1955.

————. *Survey of Major Personnel Laws Administered by the Civil Service Commission*. Washington, D.C.: U.S. Civil Service Commission, 1960.

U.S. COMMISSION ON ORGANIZATION OF THE EXECUTIVE BRANCH OF THE GOVERNMENT. *Personnel and Civil Service*. Washington, D.C.: U.S. Government Printing Office, 1955.

————. *Personnel Management*. (Report to Congress.) Washington, D.C.: U.S. Government Printing Office, 1949.

————. *Programs for Strengthening Federal Personnel Management*. (Report, with recommendations, of the Personnel Policy Committee.) Washington, D.C.: U.S. Government Printing Office, 1949.

————. *Task Force Report on Personnel and Civil Service*. Washington, D.C.: U.S. Government Printing Office, 1955.

U.S. CONGRESS. *Hearings of the House Appropriation Committee. Subcommittee on Treasury, Post Office, and Executive Offices, March 3, 1967*. Washington, D.C.: U.S. Government Printing Office, 1967.

U.S. CONGRESS, SENATE COMMITTEE ON POST OFFICE AND CIVIL SERVICE.

To Provide an Effective System of Personnel Administration. (Report of the Special Subcommittee on S. 3888.) Washington, D.C.: U.S. Government Printing Office, 1958.

―――. *To Provide an Effective System of Personnel Administration.* (Hearings, 85th Cong., 2nd Sess., on S. 3888, June, 1958.) Washington, D.C.: U.S. Government Printing Office, 1958.

―――. *To Provide for an Effective System of Personnel Administration.* (Hearings, 86th Cong., 1st Sess., on S. 1638, May, 1959.) Washington, D.C.: U.S. Government Printing Office, 1959.

―――. *Supergrades.* (Hearings, March 6, 7, 8, 11, 12, and 14, 1968.) Washington, D.C.: U.S. Government Printing Office, 1968.

VAN RIPER, PAUL P. *History of the United States Civil Service.* White Plains, N.Y.: Row, Peterson and Company, 1958.

Index

DATE DUE

PRINTED IN U.S.A

GAYLORD